כשר

KOSHER LIGHT

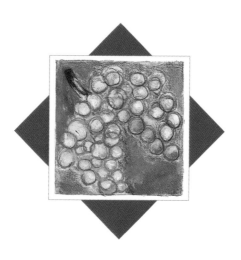

KOSHER LIGHT

YOUR
TRADITIONAL
JEWISH
FAVORITES
COOKED
HEALTHY BY
ZILLAH BAHAR

FOREWORD BY RABBI JOEL LANDAU

BETH JACOB CONGREGATION

ILLUSTRATIONS BY MARIA MAYR

PENGUIN
STUDIO

PLEASE NOTE: THIS COOKBOOK IS DESIGNED FOR THOSE WHO WISH TO RESTRICT THEIR INTAKE OF SALT, FAT, CHOLESTEROL, AND, TO A LESSER DEGREE, CALORIES. IF FURTHER REDUCTIONS ARE NECESSARY OR DESIRED, THE RECIPES HERE CAN BE EASILY ADAPTED TO LOWER LEVELS BY CONSULTING A PHYSICIAN OR A DIETICIAN. (WHEN THE CALCULATION WAS LESS THAN ONE GRAM, THE FOOD VALUE WAS RECORDED AS ZERO.) THE RECIPES IN "KOSHER LIGHT" ARE IN ACCORD WITH THE TRADITIONAL "LAWS OF KASHRUT."

PENGUIN STUDIO

PUBLISHED BY THE PENGUIN GROUP

PENGUIN PUTNAM INC., 375 HUDSON STREET,

NEW YORK, NEW YORK 10014, U. S. A.

PENGUIN BOOKS LTD, 27 WRIGHTS LANE, LONDON W8 5TZ, ENGLAND

PENGUIN BOOKS AUSTRALIA LTD, RINGWOOD, VICTORIA, AUSTRALIA

PENGUIN BOOKS CANADA LTD, 10 ALCORN AVENUE, TORONTO, ONTARIO, CANADA M4V 3B2

PENGUIN BOOKS (N.Z.) LTD, 182-190 WAIRAU ROAD, AUCKLAND 10, NEW ZEALAND

PENGUIN BOOKS LTD, REGISTERED OFFICES:

HARMONDSWORTH, MIDDLESEX, ENGLAND

FIRST PUBLISHED IN 1998 BY PENGUIN STUDIO, A MEMBER OF PENGUIN PUTNAM INC.

10   9   8   7   6   5   4   3   2   1

CIP DATA AVAILABLE

ISBN 0-670-87478-0

PRINTED IN HONG KONG

FLY
PRODUCTIONS

DEDICATION

TO
JIM
AND
SOPHIA,
MY BABY
BIRD

CONTENTS

מלכיג

MILCHIG (DAIRY) DISHES

CONTENTS

פלשיג

FLEISHIG (MEAT) DISHES

פארווארט

FOREWORD BY RABBI JOEL LANDAU

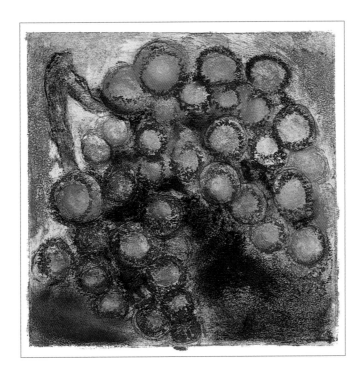

KOSHER — FOR A HEALTHIER LIFE

THE TERM KOSHER IS FAMILIAR TO EVERYONE,
but what does it really mean? Literally, kosher means "proper" or "fit," referring primarily to foods that Jewish people are permitted to eat. In the book of Leviticus, chapter 11, G-d commands the Jews, "among all the beasts that are on the earth" eat only those that have split hooves and chew their cud; of "all that are in the waters" eat only those that have fins and scales; and "among the fowls . . . shall *not* be eaten" all birds of prey.

Also crucial under kosher law is the method of slaughtering and processing the animal, fish, or fowl. Each stage of kosher food preparation is governed by strict regulations and careful supervision. Furthermore, these kosher guidelines also apply to the animals' derivatives and by-products, such as fat, oil, skin, and enzymes.

The most common misconception about kosher law is that it was instituted solely to ensure cleaner, healthier food. It's easy to see how this limited viewpoint originated, since kosher law rejects diseased animals and certain fats and bloods, affording some important hygienic benefits. In truth, however, the significance of kosher goes far deeper and is more meaningful to our lives than merely providing the framework for a healthy diet.

Although we can't possibly fathom the depth of G-d's reasoning, great Jewish thinkers throughout the ages have attempted to understand the rationale behind the kosher food laws.

One approach sees the kosher laws as a means of developing our moral and ethical behavior. The idea of using food to teach people how to behave properly began with Adam and Eve: the fruit from the Tree of Knowledge was, as we all know, forbidden to them. By considering every morsel brought to our lips in terms of right and wrong, we sensitize ourselves to become better human beings.

Another perspective on the kosher laws has to do with the development of willpower and self-discipline. By learning to say "no" to certain foods, even though tempting and tasty, we train ourselves to be less animalistic.

A third dimension comes, simply, from the observance of the laws, for by doing so, we increase our awareness of G-d's presence in the world around us. Thus the act of eating becomes an opportunity to acknowledge G-d in our midst.

Lastly, the laws of kosher represent one of the most fundamental goals of Judaism — the sanctification of the ordinary and the spiritualization of the physical. This is accomplished when food becomes not just a source of nourishment but a vehicle for holiness.

As the Scriptures state (Leviticus 11:44), "You shall be holy for I the Lord am holy."

— Rabbi Joel Landau

Beth Jacob Congregation

Irvine, California

אינטרודוקטשן

INTRODUCTION

WE SAY FOOD IS KOSHER WHEN WE MEAN THAT ITS source and preparation are in conformity with the canon of Jewish dietary laws. Anything that doesn't fall into the kosher category is considered traif: unclean, unfit to be eaten, taboo. The word kosher also takes on connotations in our vernacular that transcend its particular dietary strictures — purity, genuineness, and honesty — qualities that, not so long ago, characterized salt and fat, the foods considered to be the pillars of traditional Jewish cooking. As we learn more from doctors, scientists, newspaper articles, and television reports about how our eating habits affect our health, salt (which we once counted on to preserve our food) and fat (the age-old metaphor for abundance) lose their goodness in our minds.

And we mind very much. Today we know that the reckless consumption of both salt and fat poses a great threat to our general well-being and can lead to heart disease and cancer. Those of us who take to heart the adage that you are what you eat regard fat and salt to be as traif as a slab of bacon. Ironically, the very foods that can make us feel so good on so many levels because of their association with comfort and celebration can make us feel so bad, too. We health-conscious lovers of Jewish food, particularly dishes of Ashkenazi or Central European origin, find ourselves in a paradoxical pickle. I, for one, think that's a crime. Kosher Light is the rectification. The book transforms the salty and fatty, but beloved, Jewish favorites into wholesome dishes (without sacrificing their familiar flavors) that we can safely continue to cherish and enjoy.

The majority of the recipes I present in *Kosher Light* hail from Eastern Europe, but since my roots are Sephardic and Middle Eastern, I adapt the choice dishes from that part of the Jewish world, too. I include all our favorites: chicken soup, matzah balls (*knaidlach*), chopped chicken liver, falafel, gefilte fish with white horseradish, cheesecake, potato knish and potato pancakes (latkes), matzah brei, and the kugels — noodle (*lokshen*), potato, and matzah. A total of thirty-two recipes separated into two distinct, independent, and equal parts of the book — milchig (dairy) and fleishig (meat) — each offering starters & side dishes, main courses, and desserts.

Although dairy and meat may never be eaten together, certain foods are pareve, that is to say, neutral — made without dairy or animal products — and therefore, compatible with both dairy and meat foods (which most of the recipes in *Kosher Light* are). If you're a newcomer to the concept of kosher eating, I believe I've simplified the situation for you. When a dish in *Kosher Light* is pareve, it's indicated as such at the end of the recipe. Many of the dishes featured in the milchig section may be eaten at the same meal with fleishig offerings, and vice versa, without violating the *Laws of Kashrut*. Dishes such as beet borscht and fruit compote are pareve. Feel free to enjoy the beet borscht, a milchig starter, with stuffed cabbage, a fleishig main course; or conclude a delightful dinner of cheese blintzes, a milchig main course, with a bowl of refreshing fruit compote, a fleishig dessert. All plant foods (fruits, grains, legumes, vegetables, and their oils) are pareve. There are always exceptions to every rule and the exceptions in this case are eggs and fish. Both are pareve even though they're both animal-related foods. For the record, only fish with fins and scales are kosher; a fertilized egg is not kosher.

Keeping cholesterol and salt at bay is the imperative of *Kosher Light*. I replace all of the unhealthy ingredients with their light counterparts: I rely upon herbs and spices to replicate the traditional tastes and to enhance the flavor of the foods. Assertive seasoning makes every dish in this healthful cookbook delicious. When radical measures are called for to cook a recipe light, I take them — the use of sweet potato in the loaves of challah, for example.

Chopped chicken liver is the only recipe that requires a scant amount of salt added to kosher the liver. (The recipe guides you step-by-step through the koshering process.) You won't find a single yolk in any *Kosher Light* recipe, even in the baked desserts. I rely upon egg whites (stick with me, and you'll become an eggspert at separating) and to a lesser extent egg substitute. You won't find a pad of butter, a drop of whole milk, or a shmear of schmaltz in any *Kosher Light* recipe, either. I use the logical substitutions for these unlight ingredients: pareve unsalted margarine, low-fat or fat-free dairy products, a quick-spray of canola or olive oil, and nonstick cookware. I also recommend (and give directions for) the use of parchment paper, another method for oil-free baking. It's available in long-lasting rolls at cookware stores, most hardware stores, and by mail from specialty catalogs. The parchment paper technique works with most pans, be they springform or loaf.

A word about the salt content of the fleishig dishes in the book: The food values for the beef and poultry recipes, specifically the amount of sodium contained in a single serving, include the additional salt required to kosher the meat. Red meat is by no means a light food to begin with, but I ask you — what good would a traditional Jewish cookbook be without beef *cholent* or brisket *tzimmes*? (I did substitute ground turkey for ground beef in the stuffed cabbage, however, brisket is brisket and there's no getting around that!) My suggestion, to you fellow seekers of the light way, is savor these wonderfully familiar dishes on special occasions.

Baking Advice: Don't Let Your Wayward Oven Ruin the Cheesecake. *Kosher Light* recipes call for significantly less fat than their traditional counterparts. To insure that the baked foods, especially the pastries and cakes, turn out as good as they do in my own kitchen, I urge you to place a thermometer inside your oven for accuracy. A properly gauged oven bakes everything better.

As I kitchen-tested the recipes for *Kosher Light*, introducing new techniques and ingredients whenever I saw the need, I kept thinking about how to preserve the delicious flavor of the cuisine our beloved Jewish mothers and grandmothers created. I must confess to feeling a tinge of, well, guilt. (What else?) I don't question the rightness of making kosher food healthier. It's the key to enjoying these traditional foods more often — in some cases, at all. What I can't help but wonder is whether these wonderful Jewish women would construe my modifications of their cooking as an indictment of their dedication to our health and well-being? Would they feel unappreciated? The stories and faces of these women flash through my mind.

There's my Arabic-speaking grandmother Hanini, who was born in Baghdad and moved as a child to Bombay, where she married and raised her large family. An oval faced woman with a laugh that resounded from her belly, Hanini relished cooking the foods of her homeland. One bite into her evocative delicacies and she'd proclaim, "*Mittil Baghdad!*" (Just like in Baghdad!). How would she have felt if I told her it's better for her family to use egg substitute and part-skim cheeses in her *sambusaks* (pastry pockets)?

Then there's my friend Randy's bubbie Bella, who moved from the Ukraine to the Oxford Circle district of northeast Philadelphia. "She lived only four blocks from us, but every night my bubbie called at 5:15," recalls Randy. "I never asked who it was. I'd just say, 'Hi Grandma,' and she would ask, 'What are you eating tonight?' She needed to know."

How would Bella, for whom "schmaltz was the source of all good things," feel about using a quick-spray of canola oil instead?

These super-intelligent, hardworking women always put the health and well-being of their families first. If you consider their immigrant histories and the Jewish penchant for adapting, I don't think it's too self-serving to believe that they'd understand (and approve) the need for *Kosher Light*. After all, Jewish women always make the best of the circumstances delivered to them. And if circumstance delivers better information on how to eat and live healthfully, I don't doubt they'd want us to incorporate the knowledge into our cooking habits.

Looking at the matter from this perspective, *Kosher Light* serves as an affirmation of the beauty and goodness of the culinary traditions we inherited. It is for us, the current generation, to pick up the torch — in order to keep the cuisine of our foremothers fresh and vital — and begin to share our enlightened adaptations and inventions with each other. I welcome your thoughts and suggestions — *Kosher Light* is my contribution.

Personally, I look forward to a kosher millennium.

YOUR
TRADITIONAL
JEWISH
FAVORITES
COOKED
HEALTHY

מלביג

MILCHIG (DAIRY) DISHES

MILCHIG STARTERS & SIDE DISHES

BEET BORSCHT

GEFILTE FISH WITH WHITE HORSERADISH

FALAFEL

MUSHROOM BROTH

POTATO KNISH

FRUIT AND VEGETABLE TZIMMES

בּוּרשׁת

BEET BORSCHT

TRUE TO THE SPIRIT OF OUR THRIFTY FOREMOTHERS, IN THIS RECIPE
no part of the beet goes uneaten. The beets are baked unpeeled to preserve juice, flavor, and
nutritional value — you may come to appreciate this approach for its inherent tidiness. The
greens are wilted and spiced for garnish. The whipped egg white folded into the soup turns
this borscht a gorgeous pink color that evokes memories of the invigorating beet brew
Brooklyn bubbies served to their grandchildren on hot summer afternoons.

SERVES EIGHT

6 medium beets with tops (2 pounds)   2 quarts bottled water

2 teaspoons minced garlic   1 bunch fresh dill, snipped (½ cup)

½ cup freshly squeezed lemon juice   1 egg white

Freshly ground black pepper to taste   Olive oil spray

Preheat the oven to 325 degrees.

Scrub the beets under cold water with special attention to cleaning the sandy green
tops. Pat dry.

Slice off the beet greens, leaving 1 inch of stalk on the beet root. Cut the greens into ½-
inch pieces. Set aside.

Place the beets spaced 1 inch apart in an 11 x 7-inch nonstick baking pan. Bake the beets
in the oven for 45 minutes. Set aside to cool to room temperature.

Peel the beets. Slice into quarters and put in a food processor or blender. Coarsely grate
to yield 4 cups. Reserve ½ cup of grated beets for garnish. Set aside in an airtight container
in the refrigerator.

Combine the remaining beets, 1 teaspoon of the garlic, the lemon juice, and black pepper (to taste) in a large, heavy-bottomed pot with a tightly fitting lid, or a 5-quart Dutch oven. Add the bottled water.

Cover the pot and bring the beets to a boil. Turn the heat to low and simmer the beets for 30 minutes. Add the dill, stir, and continue to cook at a simmer for 10 minutes more. Transfer the borscht to a large bowl and set it aside, uncovered, to cool to room temperature.

Put the egg white into a medium bowl. Beat until it stands in soft peaks. Gently fold the egg white into the cooled borscht with a rubber spatula. (This is called "whiting," and it does lovely things to the texture and color of the soup.) The consistency of the borscht is best slightly thick.

Cover the bowl and place the borscht in the refrigerator to chill for 2 hours.

Quick-spray the bottom of a medium nonstick skillet with olive oil. Add the chopped beet leaves and the remaining 1 teaspoon of garlic. Sauté oven medium heat for 30 seconds to wilt the leaves and infuse them with garlicky flavor. Set the beet leaves aside to cool to room temperature.

Ladle the borscht into soup bowls, or if you want to go the old-country route, serve as a drink in a tall chilled water glass. Garnish the pretty pink soup with the greens and tea-spoon-sized dollops of ruby-red grated beets.

Store leftover beet borscht in an airtight container in the refrigerator — a glass jar with a tightly fitting lid is perfect — it keeps fresh for up to 5 days.

Beet borscht is pareve.

ONE SERVING OF BEET BORSCHT (ONE CUP) COOKED KOSHER LIGHT CONTAINS:

 20 CALORIES   ♥ 0 CHOLESTEROL   0 FAT   24 MGS SODIUM

געפילטע פיש

GEFILTE FISH WITH WHITE HORSERADISH

THE KIND OF FISH YOU USE TO PREPARE THIS QUINTESSENTIAL DISH OF Ashkenazic cuisine depends largely on where you live in the world. I use lingcod and buffalo fish, both of which are available year-round in my home state of California. If you're on the East Coast or in the Midwest, whitefish, pike, and carp — the choice of the Central Europeans who invented this dish — are more readily available. All things being equal, preferred texture should be the overriding concern when selecting the fish. Lingcod, whitefish, and even trout make a softer gefilte fish; buffalo fish and carp offer greater firmness. The accompanying recipe for horseradish produces a thoroughly macho condiment. Be especially careful as you transfer the grated horseradish from the food processor to the bowl — the vapors are overwhelming.

MAKES TWELVE FISH QUENELLES

1 fresh horseradish root (½ pound)

2 cheese cloth sacks

2 quarts plus ¾ cup bottled water

1 ½ cups thinly sliced rings plus ½ cup grated yellow onion

1 pound fish skin, bones, and heads

1 yard white cotton kitchen string

3 medium carrots, peeled

1 pound whitefish fillet

½ pound carp fillet

1 tablespoon plus 1 ½ teaspoons sugar

2 ounces egg substitute

2 tablespoons sodium-free matzah meal

1 tablespoon freshly squeezed lemon juice

1 tablespoon plus ½ teaspoon grated fresh ginger

Freshly ground black pepper to taste

Cayenne pepper to taste

1 sprig fresh tarragon

1 bay leaf

2 tablespoons white wine vinegar

2 tablespoons dry white wine

Put the horseradish root in an airtight container. Set it aside in the refrigerator for 1 hour. Chilling the horseradish takes out most of the sting from the very pungent fumes.

Fill one cheese cloth sack with the onion rings. Fill the other cheese cloth sack with the fish skin, bones, and heads. Tie the top of each sack securely closed with the kitchen string.

Put the sack of fish parts in a 12-inch skillet with a tightly fitting lid. Add the 2 quarts of water and bring to a boil. Remove the foam that forms on the surface with a slotted spoon. Add the cheese cloth sack of onions and 2 of the whole carrots to the boiling water. Lower the heat to medium and cover the skillet. Cook the fish broth at a simmer for 25 minutes. Turn off the heat. Remove the sacks of fish bones and onions and discard them. Set the broth aside.

Reserve the carrots. Slice them into ½-inch pieces and set aside.

Slice the whitefish and carp into 1-inch pieces. Double-check for tiny bones that may have been overlooked when the fish was filleted. Put the fish in a food processor or blender. Pulse to coarsely chop. Transfer the fish mixture to a large bowl.

Grate the remaining carrot into the fish mixture. Add the grated onion, 1 ½ teaspoons of the sugar, egg substitute, matzah meal, lemon juice, ½ teaspoon of the grated ginger, and the black pepper and cayenne pepper (to taste). Stir the batter vigorously, distributing the ingredients evenly throughout. The consistency of the fish batter is best lumpy.

Into the skillet of broth, add the tarragon sprig and the bay leaf. Cover and bring to a boil. Lower the heat to medium to slow the broth to a bubbling simmer.

Spoon out ¼ cup of the fish batter. Shape it into a ball about 3 ½ inches across. Flatten the fish ball slightly. Use a slotted spoon to place it in the simmering broth. Repeat this process with the remaining batter to yield 12 gefilte fish quenelles.

Lower the heat, cover the skillet, and cook at a simmer for 20 minutes. The gefilte fish are done when they expand slightly and are firm to the touch.

Lift the gefilte fish and the carrots out of the broth with a slotted spoon. Set them aside on a large platter to cool to room temperature.

Put the broth in a large airtight container and set it aside, uncovered, to cool to room temperature.

Into the container of room-temperature broth, put the gefilte fish and the sliced carrots. Cover and set aside in the refrigerator to chill for 2 hours.

To make the horseradish: Remove the horseradish from the refrigerator. Peel the horseradish and cut it into 2-inch slices. Put the slices into a food processor or blender. Coarsely grate to yield 1½ cups.

Using great care to protect your eyes and throat from horseradish vapors, transfer the grated horseradish to a large bowl. Add the remaining 1 tablespoon of sugar, the vinegar, the remaining 1 tablespoon of grated ginger, the white wine, and the remaining ¾ cup bottled water. Stir the mixture vigorously, distributing the ingredients evenly throughout.

Serve each diner 1 chilled gefilte fish with some carrots and jellied broth spooned on top. A generous tablespoon-size dollop of horseradish on each plate is plenty for a bracing duo like you've never tasted!

Store the fiery horseradish and the gefilte fish in separate airtight containers in the refrigerator. The gefilte fish keep for 1 week; the horseradish keeps indefinitely.

Gefilte fish and white horseradish are both pareve.

ONE SERVING OF GEFILTE FISH (ONE QUENELLE AND ONE TABLESPOON OF HORSERADISH) COOKED KOSHER LIGHT CONTAINS:

 92 CALORIES  32 MGS CHOLESTEROL  3 GMS FAT  33 MGS SODIUM

פאלאפל

FALAFEL

IN ISRAEL, FALAFEL ARE THE FAST FOOD OF CHOICE, WITH AS MANY variations on the spicy round croquette as there are neighborhood restaurants that serve them. This Middle Eastern street food is deep-fried in oil to crunchy perfection. While my variety is a stove-top sauté cooked kosher light, the little fritters are crispy nonetheless.

MAKES EIGHTEEN FRITTERS

½ can (7 ¼ ounces) garbanzo beans, drained and rinsed (¾ cup)

⅔ cup bottled water

3 ½ ounces dried bulgur wheat (½ cup)

1 tablespoon Roasted Garlic (page 56)

2 tablespoons minced yellow onion

1 teaspoon ground cumin

2 sprigs fresh cilantro, minced (2 tablespoons)

3 egg whites

Freshly ground black pepper to taste

Cayenne pepper to taste

Olive oil spray

½ teaspoon freshly squeezed lemon juice

Put the garbanzo beans into a small bowl. Add cold water to cover and set the beans aside to soak for 10 minutes. Drain in a sieve and rinse under cold water. Pat dry.

Puree the garbanzos in a food processor or blender. Set aside.

Bring the bottled water to a boil.

Into a medium bowl, put the bulgur wheat. Add the boiling water and stir. Cover the bowl and set aside for 30 minutes until the bulgur wheat absorbs all the water.

Into the bowl of parcooked bulgur wheat, add the pureed garbanzos, roasted garlic, onion, cumin, and cilantro. Stir to mix well. Fold in the egg whites. Sprinkle the black pepper and cayenne pepper over all (to taste) and mix thoroughly. The falafel batter is the consistency of oatmeal. Yields 2 cups.

Quick-spray the bottom of a 12-inch non-stick skillet with olive oil. Preheat the pan over low heat.

Spoon out 1 tablespoon of falafel batter. Shape it into a ball about 1 ½ inches across. Place the ball of batter into the pre-heated pan. Gently flatten the fritter to a ½-inch thickness. Cook the falafel in 2 batches — the pan accommodates 9 falafel spaced ½ inch apart. Sprinkle the fritters with lemon juice. Repeat the process with the remaining batter to yield 18 falafel fritters.

Raise the heat to medium. Sauté the falafel for 7 minutes until they're crisp and brown. Turn them over and sauté 5 minutes more. The falafel fritters are done when they puff up slightly and are crispy brown on both sides. Transfer to a covered plate and set aside.

Repeat the process to cook the second batch of falafel.

Coupled with crudités, falafel are perfect finger-food starters to whet the appetite before dinner and stand in deliciously as a side dish with baked salmon or brisket tzimmes (instead of the expected rice or broad noodles). The condiment of choice to complement this Middle Eastern classic is a fiery dipping sauce. These little fritters are versatile (and pareve).

Falafel keep in the refrigerator for 3 days stored in an airtight container. To serve as leftovers — they make a great light lunch — allow them to return to room temperature, slice them into bite-sized pieces, and toss them into a green salad instead of croutons.

Falafel are pareve.

ONE SERVING OF FALAFEL (THREE FRITTERS) COOKED KOSHER LIGHT CONTAINS:

 38 CALORIES   ♥ 0 CHOLESTEROL   0 FAT    24 MGS SODIUM

מַשְׁרוּם זוּפּ

MUSHROOM BROTH

WHEN YOU'RE FEELING UNDER THE WEATHER, THERE'S NOTHING LIKE mushroom broth thickened with pureed carrots and mushrooms to invigorate you, body and soul. Very simple; very comforting. You'll like the broth even more as you discover its versatility, especially as the main ingredient in fat-free gravy or as the base for the *Kosher Light* lentil soup with mushrooms. Paired with veggies such as eggplant and roasted peppers, it transforms a homely bowl of legumes into a substantial gourmet meal. Use mushroom broth as a healthful yet richly flavored substitute for heavy beef broth in other recipes, too.

SERVES EIGHT (MAKES EIGHT CUPS)

2 quarts plus 1 cup bottled water	4 sprigs fresh thyme
1 ½ ounces loosely packed, dried whole porcini mushrooms (1 cup)	4 sprigs fresh flat-leaf parsley
	1 sprig fresh rosemary
Olive oil spray	2 tablespoons dry red wine
¾ cup coarsely chopped yellow onion	Freshly ground black pepper to taste
3 medium carrots, peeled and cut into ½-inch rounds (1 ½ cups)	¼ cup snipped fresh chives for garnish

Bring 1 cup of bottled water to a boil.

Rinse the mushrooms under cold water. Put them into a medium bowl. Add the boiling water, cover, and set aside for 20 minutes to rehydrate the mushrooms.

Quick-spray the bottom of a large, heavy-bottomed pot with a tightly fitting lid, or a 5-quart Dutch oven with olive oil. Add the chopped onion. Sauté over low heat for 2 to 3 minutes, until the onion begins to soften. Add the carrots, thyme, parsley, rosemary, and red wine. Stir.

Raise the heat to medium and sauté for 2 or 3 minutes more until the wine evaporates and the onion begins to turn golden.

Add the 2 quarts of bottled water and the mushrooms, including their rehydrating liquid. Stir to mix well. Cover, raise the heat to medium-high, and bring to a boil.

Lower the heat to medium and cook the broth at a bubbling simmer for 30 minutes until the mushrooms and carrots are tender. Set aside to cool to room temperature.

Strain the broth through a colander into a large bowl. Reserve the carrots and ¼ cup of the mushrooms. Discard the chopped onion and the herbs.

Put the carrots, mushrooms, and 1 cup of the broth into a food processor or blender. Puree the mixture to a smooth consistency.

Return the pureed mushrooms and carrots to the broth. Stir to completely combine. Taste and season with one or two grinds from a pepper mill, if you like.

Serve the mushroom broth steaming hot with a garnish of snipped chives.

Mushroom broth keeps for 5 days in an airtight container in the refrigerator. Feel free to freeze several cups of the mushroom broth in individual ice cube molds to use on the spur of the moment to flavor stews, soups, dips, and sauces. Frozen in this way, the mushroom broth keeps indefinitely.

Mushroom broth is pareve.

THE FUNGUS AMONG US JEWS: The Jewish cooks of Eastern Europe favored boletus mushrooms (also known as cepes in France or porcini in Italy) to fill kreplach and to mix with kasha. Mushroom gathering in the woods and fields surrounding small villages was one of the few events interesting enough to draw Jewish men away from their Talmudic studies. The mushrooms were collected, sundried, strung on twine, and stored in jars to flavor wintertime soups and stews.

ONE SERVING OF MUSHROOM BROTH (ONE CUP) COOKED KOSHER LIGHT CONTAINS:

 26 CALORIES   0 CHOLESTEROL 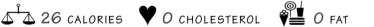 0 FAT  3 MGS SODIUM

קניש

POTATO KNISH

EPITOMIZING JEWISH COMFORT FOOD AT ITS BEST, DELICIOUS KNISH come out of the oven looking like little golden cushions. Flecks of rosemary and threads of saffron decorate the delicate biscuit shells. Shallots and a dash of nutmeg season the mashed potato and mushroom filling with savory warmth. Serve them to *mishpocheh* as a token of unflagging affection (sealed with a knish).

MAKES FOUR KNISH

½ medium yellowfin potato (¼ pound)	Pinch saffron threads
1 tablespoon pareve unsalted margarine	Olive oil spray
½ cup flour	¼ cup minced shallot
⅛ teaspoon baking soda	3 medium white mushrooms, thinly sliced (¼ cup)
½ teaspoon low-sodium baking powder	
2 ½ tablespoons plus 1 tablespoon nonfat plain yogurt	Pinch ground nutmeg
	1 egg white
¼ teaspoon minced fresh rosemary	Freshly ground black pepper to taste

Scrub the potato under cold water. Remove the peel and slice in half.

Put 4 cups of water into a medium pot and bring to a boil. Add the potato. Boil for 8 to 10 minutes until the potato is soft and cooked through. Transfer the potato to a plate to cool to room temperature.

Mash the potato and set it aside. Yields ½ cup.

Cut the margarine into ½-inch pieces.

Sift the flour, baking soda, and baking powder together into a medium bowl.

14

Put the margarine and the flour mixture into a food processor. Process to just incorporate. The consistency of the mixture resembles coarse bread crumbs.

Add 2 ½ tablespoons of the yogurt, the rosemary, and saffron. Process to just incorporate. The consistency of the batter is best lumpy. Cover and set aside to chill in the refrigerator for 15 minutes.

Quick-spray the bottom of a medium non-stick pan with olive oil. Add the shallots, mushrooms, and nutmeg. Sauté over medium heat for 3 or 4 minutes, until the mushrooms soften and the shallots become translucent. Set the mushroom sauté aside to cool to room temperature.

Put the mashed potato, the remaining 1 tablespoon of yogurt, and the egg white into a blender. Blend for 30 seconds until smooth.

Transfer the potato mixture to a medium bowl. Add the mushroom sauté and a grind of black pepper (to taste). Stir the knish filling to evenly distribute all of the ingredients.

Preheat the oven to 375 degrees.

Line a 10 x 14-inch baking sheet with parchment paper.

Remove the dough from the refrigerator. Place it on a floured board and divide it into 4 equal portions. Shape each portion into a ball. Flatten each ball of dough into a circle 5 inches across and ¼ inch thick.

Place 1 heaping tablespoon of knish filling into the center of the circle. Lift the edges of the circle, gather them together, pinch them closed – sealing in the filling – to make a bundle 3 inches across. The filled knish resembles a little cushion.

Repeat this process to fill the remaining 3 circles of dough for a total of 4 knish.

Place the knish, pinched-side up, spaced 1 ½ inches apart on the baking sheet. Bake in the oven for 20 minutes until the knish expand slightly and turn a light, golden brown.

Potato knish keep for 2 days stored in an airtight container in the refrigerator.

ONE SERVING OF POTATO KNISH (ONE KNISH) COOKED KOSHER LIGHT CONTAINS:

86 CALORIES   ♥ 0 CHOLESTEROL    2 GMS FAT   48 MGS SODIUM

צימעס

FRUIT AND VEGETABLE TZIMMES

TZIMMES, LIKE CHOLENT, IS AN OLD-COUNTRY RECIPE HANDED down from mother to daughter. It's hearty, tasty, healthy, and idiosyncratic. Every family has its own version. My tzimmes is a sweet-and-sour variation on the main theme: baked vegetables and fruits. These days, food gurus and celebrity MDs tout the super-nutritious benefits of combining carbs and proteins, something our unscientific bubbies did instinctively. (Yam and potato don their protein hats to make the point.)

SERVES FOUR

1 medium navel orange

3 tablespoons Madeira wine

½ teaspoon minced orange zest

1 tablespoon honey

2 ounces pitted prunes, cut in half (¼ cup)

2 ounces dried apricots, cut in half (¼ cup)

¾ cup bottled water

Olive oil spray

1 cup coarsely chopped yellow onion

1 teaspoon balsamic vinegar

1 yam (½ pound), cut into ¼-inch rounds (1 cup)

1 Idaho potato (½ pound), cut into ¼-inch rounds (1 cup)

4 baby carrots, peeled and cut into ¼-inch rounds (1 cup)

Cayenne pepper to taste

Peel, devein, and divide the orange into sections. Slice the orange sections into bite-sized pieces in a large bowl to collect the orange juice. Yields 1 cup. Set aside.

In a small saucepan, combine the Madeira wine, orange zest, and honey. Stir to mix. Over very low heat, warm the spiced wine, stirring frequently, for 2 minutes until the honey is completely dissolved. Remove the saucepan from the heat and set aside.

Into the bowl of chopped orange and its juice, add the prunes and apricots. Toss to combine. Pour the zesty, sweetened wine over all. Stir to coat well. Add the bottled water. Stir to incorporate. Cover and set the wine and fruit mixture aside for 30 minutes.

Quick-spray the bottom of a large non-stick skillet with a tightly fitting lid with olive oil. Preheat the skillet over low heat. Add the chopped onion. Sauté for 3 minutes over a low heat until the onions turn translucent. Add the balsamic vinegar and continue sautéing for 2 minutes more until the onions begin to brown. Remove the sautéed onion from the skillet and set aside.

Put the yam, potato, and carrots into the skillet. Raise the heat to medium and cook for 5 minutes, toss-stirring, until the sliced vegetables are lightly browned on all sides.

Lower the heat and return the onions to the skillet. Toss with the vegetables. Add the fruit mixture and its zesty liquid. Stir to coat all the ingredients. Sprinkle cayenne over all (to taste) and stir. Cover the skillet and slowly simmer the tzimmes for 10 minutes until the fruits and vegetables begin to soften. Turn off the heat and set aside.

Preheat the oven to 325 degrees.

Quick-spray the bottom of a large non-stick covered casserole or baking dish with olive oil. Transfer the tzimmes and its flavorful juice to the casserole. Toss to mix and cover.

Bake in the oven for 1 hour and 20 minutes. Every 30 minutes, give the tzimmes a stir. The tzimmes is done when the fruit is soft and the vegetables are tender.

Fruit and vegetable tzimmes tastes best served at room temperature. The savory-sweet tzimmes is a satisfyingly substantial side dish for baked salmon and is surprisingly successful paired with matzah brei — something about the combination of sweet softness and savory crispness makes these two unlikely partners the perfect match.

Fruit and vegetable tzimmes keeps in the refrigerator for 3 to 4 days stored in an air-tight container.

Fruit and vegetable tzimmes is pareve.

ONE SERVING OF FRUIT AND VEGETABLE TZIMMES (ONE CUP) COOKED KOSHER LIGHT CONTAINS:

133 CALORIES   **0** CHOLESTEROL   **0** FAT   **7** MGS SODIUM

MILCHIG MAIN COURSES

BAKED SALMON

CHEESE BLINTZES

LENTIL SOUP WITH MUSHROOMS

MATZAH BREI

POTATO PANCAKES (LATKES)

באיקד סעמען

BAKED SALMON

WHY IS SALMON A TRADITIONAL JEWISH FISH? SIMPLE AVAILABILITY is probably the answer. Like her kosher sisters, herring and carp, salmon swims the cold ocean waters of the North Sea and the Northern Atlantic. The delicate pink flesh should never be over-seasoned; salmon's natural flavor is a great pleasure in and of itself. A quick stopover in a lemony spice marinade emphasizes the sweetness of the fish by giving a mouth-watering tartness to the cooking juices. Baked on a bed of fresh baby peas and wilted scallions — Italian-Jewish style — adds texture and a touch of green to this lovely dish.

SERVES FOUR

1 teaspoon minced fresh tarragon	4 salmon fillets, 4 ounces each
3 tablespoons freshly squeezed lemon juice	½ pound fresh green peas, shelled (½ cup)
3 tablespoons bottled water	¼ cup julienne-sliced scallions
Pinch cardamom seeds, crushed	Freshly ground black pepper to taste
Pinch cayenne pepper	

In a small bowl, combine the minced tarragon, lemon juice, water, crushed cardamom seeds, and cayenne pepper. Stir to mix. Set the seasoned liquid aside for 20 minutes to allow the flavors of the moistened spices to develop into an aromatic marinade.

Preheat the oven to 400 degrees.

Pour the marinade into an 11 x 7-inch nonstick baking dish with a tightly fitting lid. Spread the liquid to coat the bottom of the dish. Place the salmon fillets in the shallow liquid, turning them over once or twice to coat both sides evenly with flavor. Cover and set aside to maturate in the refrigerator for 10 minutes. The spices are bold — the idea is to add interest to the unique flavor of the salmon, not bury it.

Remove the baking dish from the refrigerator. Transfer the fillets to a plate and set aside.

Put the fresh peas into the baking dish and spread them in an even layer to cover the bottom. Scatter the sliced scallions over the peas. Return the salmon fillets to the baking dish to cook perched atop the bed of peas and scallions. Cover the baking dish.

Bake the salmon in the oven for 15 minutes. It's not necessary to turn the fillets over. The delicate flesh cooks through quickly in the hot oven. To test for doneness, gently pierce the salmon with a fork. If the fork slides in and out easily, the fish is ready.

Present each diner with a salmon fillet and a garnish of savory baked peas and scallions. This main course goes beautifully with an accompaniment of fragrant *Kosher Light* potato knish. The finish to this splendid meal should be nothing more elaborate than a trim slice of poppy seed cake, cooked the light way, naturally.

Baked salmon is pareve.

A FISH STORY. OR, MAY YOU BE FISH-FUL AND MULTIPLY: Sephardic folklore links fish to fertility. Moroccan newlyweds host a fish dinner for family and friends shortly after their wedding. During the meal, the groom takes a ceremonial bite of fish and his bride steps over a fishnet. Similarly, brides hop over plates of fish at Jewish wedding feasts in Sarajevo and the Greek city of Salonika. These fishy rituals are performed to "insure" pregnancy, early and often.

ONE SERVING OF BAKED SALMON (FOUR-OUNCE FILLET) COOKED KOSHER LIGHT CONTAINS:

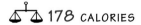 **178** CALORIES   ♥ **63** MGS CHOLESTEROL   **5** GMS FAT   **67** MGS SODIUM

בלינצים

CHEESE BLINTZES

THE FILLING FOR THESE BLINTZES TASTES TERRIFICALLY CHEESY,

although you use a sparse three-quarters cup of part-skim ricotta for the entire recipe. The addition of whipped egg whites in the filling makes these blintzes virtually buoyant. They come out of the oven toasty brown and all puffed up like little pillows. Omit the traditional sour cream accompaniment and top these light blintzes with an aromatic garnish of fresh spearmint for a Sephardic touch.

MAKES EIGHT BLINTZES

6 ounces egg substitute

1 tablespoon plus 1 teaspoon freshly squeezed orange juice

¼ teaspoon grated orange zest

1 plus ½ teaspoon vanilla extract

¼ cup cold bottled water

¼ cup skim milk

⅓ cup flour

¼ teaspoon cornstarch

⅛ teaspoon ground nutmeg

Canola oil spray

8 sheets (9-inch square) parchment paper

¾ container (6 ounces) part-skim ricotta cheese (¾ cup)

1 tablespoon sugar

3 egg whites

2 tablespoons minced fresh spearmint for garnish

In a food processor or blender, combine the egg substitute, 1 teaspoon of the orange juice, the orange zest, ½ teaspoon of the vanilla extract, cold bottled water, and the skim milk. Process to blend.

Sift the flour, cornstarch, and nutmeg together into a medium bowl.

Add the flour mixture to the wet ingredients in the food processor or blender. Process to blend. The consistency of the blintz skin batter is best thin and silky-smooth. Yields about 2 cups.

Quick-spray the bottom of a 9-inch crepe pan with canola oil. Preheat the pan over low heat.

Place a large platter and the stack of parchment paper within easy reach of the stove. Put 1 square of paper on the plate.

Give the batter a swift stir and pour a scant ¼ cup into the bottom of the heated pan. Tilt the pan to coat the bottom completely with an even layer of batter. Cover and cook for 2 minutes. Uncover and continue to cook for 2 minutes more until the edges of the blintz skin turn light brown and begin to curl.

With a spatula, carefully lift the blintz skin out of the pan. Set it aside on the square of paper. Place a second sheet on top.

Repeat this process with the remaining batter to yield 8 blintz skins.

Preheat the oven to 350 degrees.

Quick-spray the bottom of a 14 x 16-inch baking sheet with canola oil.

Wash and dry the food processor or blender.

To make the blintz filling: Put the ricotta, the sugar, 1 tablespoon of the orange juice, and 1 teaspoon of the vanilla extract into the food processor or blender. Process to blend. Continue to pulse-blend the filling to a smooth, creamy texture.

Put the egg whites into a large bowl. Beat until they stand in soft peaks. Use a rubber spatula to fold the egg whites into the blintz filling.

Place 2 heaping tablespoons of filling into the center of a blintz skin, cooked-side up. Fold in the sides of the blintz skin to overlap each other and enclose the filling to make an envelope-shaped cheese blintz about 3 inches square. Place the blintz on the baking sheet, seam-side down.

Repeat this process with the remaining 7 blintzes. The baking sheet accommodates eight cheese blintzes, spaced 1 inch apart.

Quick-spritz the tops of the blintzes with canola oil. Bake the blintzes in the oven for 15 minutes. The blintzes are done when they puff up and the tops turn a soft, toasty brown.

The cunning flavor of spearmint makes a most inviting garnish. Sprinkle ¼ teaspoon of minced mint on each blintz and — serve 'em hot — 1 to a customer.

Cheese blintzes don't store well in the refrigerator, although you probably won't have leftovers to worry about. Even wrapped tightly in an airtight container in the refrigerator, they're good for only 24 hours.

DAIRY DEVOTEES: In Yiddish, blintzes are bletlach, or skeleton leaves, a reference to the thin pastry that envelopes the creamy filling. Blintzes are served on Shavuot, the holiday honoring the gift of the Ten Commandments. The observant forgo meat on the first day of this two day celebration. Legend tells us, the Hebrews were so eager to leave Mount Sinai and begin their journey to the land of milk and honey, they had no time to kosher their meat, and thus, the tradition of milchig during Shavuot.

ONE SERVING OF CHEESE BLINTZES (ONE BLINTZ) BAKED KOSHER LIGHT CONTAINS:

 49 CALORIES ♥ 2 MGS CHOLESTEROL   0 FAT  61 MGS SODIUM

לינטעל זופּ

LENTIL SOUP WITH MUSHROOMS

THOSE OF US WHO'VE GROWN UP WITH SEPHARDIC- AND MIDDLE
Eastern-style home cooking know (and rely upon) the piquant chili pepper as a valuable
flavor enhancer. Serrano chili lends a vibrancy to this very thick lentil soup with mushrooms
that's unattainable with salt. (I'm not just offering you a nondescript bowl of beans.) A
garnish with savor is the succulent combination of eggplant and roasted red bell pepper —
the Sephardic cousin to ratatouille — served on top of each portion.

SERVES EIGHT

Olive oil spray

2 tablespoons pressed garlic

¼ pound white mushrooms, thinly sliced (1 cup)

6 cups Mushroom Broth (page 12)

¾ can (10 ½ ounces) low-sodium tomato puree (1 ½ cups)

1 serrano chili, coarsely chopped (¼ cup)

12 ½ ounces dried lentils (2 cups)

3 medium carrots, peeled and thinly sliced (1 ¼ cups)

Freshly ground black pepper to taste

1 medium red bell pepper

1 medium Italian eggplant, thinly sliced (2 cups)

Quick-spray the bottom of a medium nonstick skillet with olive oil. Add 1 tablespoon of the
garlic and the sliced mushrooms. Stir to mix. Sauté over medium heat for 2 minutes until the
mushrooms begin to wilt and soften. Transfer the garlic-flavored mushrooms into a small
bowl and set aside.

In a large, heavy-bottomed pot with a tightly fitting lid, or a 5-quart Dutch oven, combine
the mushroom broth, tomato puree, serrano chili, and the remaining 1 tablespoon of garlic.

Cover and bring to a boil. Lower the heat and add the lentils. Cover the pot and cook at a simmer, stirring frequently, for 30 minutes.

Add the carrots, softened mushrooms, and black pepper (to taste). Stir to combine with the simmering beans. Raise the heat to medium and cook the soup at a bubbling simmer for 15 minutes more until the lentils are tender and the texture of the soup is thick and chunky. To test for doneness, remove a spoonful of beans and blow on them. If the skins burst, consider them properly cooked.

While the soup is cooking, prepare the eggplant and roasted red bell pepper garnish.

Preheat the broiler.

Cut the bell pepper in half lengthwise. Remove the veins and seeds. Quick-spray both sides of each bell pepper half with olive oil.

Place the bell pepper halves spaced 2 inches apart on a 10 x 14-inch baking sheet, skin-side up. Broil for 8 to 12 minutes until the skins are charred and blistered. Set aside to cool to room temperature.

Remove the charred skins and julienne slice the roasted pepper halves. Set aside.

Quick-spray the bottom of the medium nonstick skillet with olive oil. Add the sliced eggplant. Sauté over medium heat for 7 minutes. Turn the slices over and sauté for 5 to 7 minutes more until the eggplant is a crispy golden brown. Remove the skillet from the heat and allow the eggplant to cool slightly. Add the roasted pepper halves and stir to combine with the eggplant. Yields about 2 ¼ cups.

Transfer the eggplant and roasted red bell pepper garnish to a bowl and set aside.

Present the lentil soup with mushrooms in deep soup bowls. Garnish each portion with a generous dollop of eggplant and roasted red bell pepper.

Lentil soup with mushrooms is pareve.

ONE SERVING OF LENTIL SOUP WITH MUSHROOMS (ONE-AND-ONE-HALF CUPS) COOKED KOSHER LIGHT CONTAINS:

 161 CALORIES  0 CHOLESTEROL   1 GM FAT  20 MGS SODIUM

מצה בראי

MATZAH BREI

PESACH BREAKFAST CLASSIC — THE JEWISH VERSION OF HASH BROWNS
is prepared by frying a mixture of eggs and softened matzah. Some people like it flavored sweetly
with a sprinkling of sugar and cinnamon. I prefer it savory. The *Kosher Light* version with onions
gives me a new appreciation for the taste and versatility of egg whites, which are the key to
crisp, satisfying matzah brei. Using just the whites in the matzah brei batter produces a fluffy
texture that's impossible to achieve with whole eggs and turns this cholesterol-rich dish
kosher light.

SERVES FOUR

4 sodium-free matzahs	Canola oil spray
4 egg whites	1 cup coarsely chopped yellow onion
Pinch cayenne pepper	2 tablespoons snipped fresh chives
Freshly ground black pepper to taste	for garnish

Put the matzahs into a large nonreactive baking pan. Add water to cover, about 3 cups. Set
aside to soak for 3 minutes until the matzahs are soft and flexible. Discard the unabsorbed
water and dry the pan.

Place half the softened matzah into a fine-meshed sieve. Use the back of a large spoon to
press out the excess water. The drained matzah paste is the consistency of cooked oatmeal.
Put the matzah paste into the dry pan. Repeat this process for the remaining softened
matzah. Yields about 3 cups.

Add the egg whites to the matzah paste. Stir to mix well. Sprinkle cayenne and black
pepper (to taste) over all and stir. Continue to stir the matzah paste until it thickens into a

stiff batter. Set the matzah batter aside.

Quick-spray the bottom of a medium nonstick skillet with canola oil.

Preheat the skillet over medium heat.

Add the chopped onion and lower the heat. Sauté for about 5 minutes until the onion turns translucent.

Pour the matzah batter into the skillet. Stir to distribute the onions. Cook the matzah brei for 3 to 4 minutes until it becomes firm and begins to brown. Scramble the matzah brei with a nonstick spatula to prevent it from sticking to the bottom of the skillet. Cook, stirring, for 1 to 2 minutes more. The matzah brei is done when it turns light golden brown and very crispy.

Hot and crunchy, garnished with snipped fresh chives, matzah brei makes a great dieter's lunch beside a salad of tart beets.

Matzah brei is pareve.

PUTTING A DAMPER ON BREAKFAST: Matzah brei means "soaked matzah" in Yiddish. The matzah may be softened in milk or water. The traditional way is in water to keep the matzah pareve, since Ashkenazim (creators of this Jewish comfort-food classic) use chicken fat to fry the matzah brei. Either way you soak it, the truly cautious don't make matzah brei on Passover out of concern that moistened matzah may ferment and violate the dietary strictures of eating only unleavened bread on Pesach.

ONE SERVING OF MATZAH BREI COOKED KOSHER LIGHT CONTAINS:

 135 CALORIES   0 CHOLESTEROL    0 FAT    41 MGS SODIUM

לאטקעס

POTATO PANCAKES (LATKES)

BAKED LIGHT WITH A DASH OF OIL, THESE LATKES ARE JUST AS CRISPY
and golden brown as the traditional pan-fried variety. Whither the salt? You'll be loving them
too much to care. Crackling onions, pungent shallots, and cheeky cayenne make these latkes
a super-savory holiday specialty to look forward to each year as Chanukkah or Passover
approaches. Prepared with a binding of egg whites, they're a lacy, feather-light delight — and
that's no yolk.

MAKES TWENTY-FIVE LATKES

1 Idaho potato (1 pound)	Freshly ground black pepper to taste
2 egg whites	Pinch cayenne pepper
2 tablespoons sodium-free matzah meal	¼ teaspoon pressed garlic
¾ cup coarsely chopped yellow onion	Canola oil spray
¼ cup coarsely chopped shallot	

Preheat the oven to 400 degrees.

Put a 14 x 16-inch nonstick baking sheet into the oven to preheat.

Scrub the potato under cold water. Peel and slice into quarters. Put the slices of potato
into a food processor or blender. Coarsely grate to yield 1 ¾ cups.

Pour ½ cup of the grated potato into a fine-meshed sieve. Place the sieve over a small
bowl and, using the back of a large spoon, press the water out of the grated potato into the
bowl. (Removing the water from the grated potato is the secret behind crispy latkes.) Empty
the sieve of dehydrated potato into a second bowl. Repeat this process for the remaining
grated potato.

Set the bowl of potato water aside for 5 minutes to allow the potato starch to sink to the bottom.

Into the bowl of grated potato, add the egg whites, matzah meal, onion, shallot, black pepper, cayenne pepper, and garlic. Stir the batter vigorously, distributing the ingredients evenly throughout. Mix to just combine — the consistency of the batter is best lumpy.

Now, turn your attention to the bowl of reserved potato water. Carefully pour off the water to reveal about 1 tablespoon of starch at the bottom of the bowl. Scoop up the starch with a spoon and add it to the latke batter. Mix to incorporate. (The potato starch is a leavening agent like baking powder to make the latkes cook light as a feather.)

Remove the baking sheet from the oven. Quick-spray the surface with canola oil. Drop rounded tablespoons of batter onto the baking sheet, spaced ½ inch apart. Gently flatten the latkes to about 2 ½ inches across by ⅛ inch thick. The baking sheet accommodates 12 or 13 latkes arranged in this way. Cook the latkes in 2 batches.

Bake the latkes in the oven for 10 minutes. Turn them over and bake for 5 minutes more. The latkes are cooked to perfection when they're golden brown and crispy. Transfer to a covered plate and set aside.

Repeat the process for the second batch of latkes.

Present the piping hot potato pancakes, stacked pyramid style, on a warmed platter. Serve just-light with individual bowls of tart and sweet applesauce, if you wish.

Potato latkes are pareve and kosher for Passover.

ONE SERVING OF POTATO PANCAKES (SIX LATKES) BAKED KOSHER LIGHT CONTAINS:

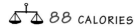 88 CALORIES    0 CHOLESTEROL   0 FAT    27 MGS SODIUM

MILCHIG DESSERTS

CHEESECAKE

HAMANTASCHEN

POPPY SEED CAKE

NOODLE KUGEL

MARBLED POUND CAKE

טשיעז קייק

CHEESECAKE

USING HOMEMADE NONFAT YOGURT CHEESE IN COMBINATION
with a little part-skim ricotta cuts cholesterol while maintaining the creamy texture we've
come to adore in cheesecake. Never mind if you've never made yogurt cheese before. Draining
the liquid from yogurt to make cheese is an age-old Middle Eastern technique. All you do is
fill cheese cloth sacks with yogurt and suspend them over the kitchen sink — you'll get the
hang of it! A crumbly spice-cookie bottom featuring lemon zest and ginger is the finishing
touch to this tart dessert tailored to grown-up palates.

SERVES TWELVE (MAKES ONE TEN-INCH CAKE)

2 containers (32 ounces each) nonfat natural yogurt

2 cheese cloth sacks

1 yard of white cotton kitchen string

1 sheet (18-inch square) parchment paper

4 tablespoons pareve unsalted margarine

⅔ cup plus 3 tablespoons sugar

2 tablespoons packed brown sugar

1 tablespoon molasses

5 egg whites

2 teaspoons vanilla extract

1 teaspoon plus ¾ teaspoon grated lemon zest

1 cup sifted flour

½ teaspoon baking soda

¼ teaspoon cream of tartar

½ teaspoon ground cinnamon

¼ teaspoon ground cloves

¼ teaspoon ground nutmeg

¾ teaspoons ground ginger

2 teaspoons freshly squeezed orange juice

1 tablespoon cornstarch

¾ container (6 ounces) part-skim ricotta cheese (¾ cup)

35

Fill each cheese cloth sack with 1 container of yogurt. Tie the top of each sack securely closed with kitchen string. Make a loop with the string long enough to suspend each sack from the kitchen sink faucet. It takes 8 to 12 hours for all of the liquid in the yogurt to slowly drain out of the sacks. For the sake of convenience, plan to let them hang overnight.

Untie the sacks and spoon the yogurt cheese into a large bowl. It yields about 2 ½ cups. Set it aside in the refrigerator while you prepare the cake bottom.

To make the cake bottom: Preheat the oven to 375 degrees. Release the bottom of a 10-inch springform pan from its sides. Trace the bottom on a sheet of parchment paper and cut out the paper circle. Dampen one side of the circle with a few drops of water. Place it into the bottom of the pan damp-side down. Reassemble the spring-form pan.

Into a food processor or blender, put the margarine, 3 tablespoons of the granulated sugar, brown sugar, molasses, 1 egg white, 1 teaspoon of the vanilla extract, and 1 teaspoon of the grated lemon zest. Process to blend.

Sift the flour, baking soda, cream of tartar, cinnamon, cloves, nutmeg, and ginger together into a medium bowl.

Add the flour mixture to the wet ingredients in the food processor or blender and process to just blend. The pastry batter is caramel colored. The consistency is thick and sticky.

Drop teaspoons of batter into the springform pan, but don't let the sticky batter touch the sides of the pan. Smooth out the surface of the batter with the back of a wet teaspoon.

Bake the pastry bottom in the oven for 12 minutes. Rotate the pan 180 degrees and bake for 13 minutes more until the cake bottom turns a deep honey color and is firm to the touch. Set aside to cool for 1 hour.

To make the cake filling: Preheat the oven to 325 degrees. In a large bowl, combine the remaining 1 teaspoon of vanilla extract and the orange juice. Stir to incorporate. Add the cornstarch and stir to dissolve. Add the yogurt cheese, the remaining ⅔ cup sugar, the remaining ¾ teaspoon lemon zest, and the ricotta. Mix the filling to evenly distribute all of the ingredients.

Put the remaining 4 egg whites into the work bowl of a mixer. Beat them until they stand in soft peaks. Fold the egg whites into the yogurt cheese mixture with a rubber spatula in 2 additions. The cake filling is the consistency of thick yogurt.

Cut out strips of parchment paper wide enough to cover the sides of the springform pan. Dampen one side of each strip with a few drops of water. Place them, damp-side down, to cover the sides of the pan. Pour the filling over the cake bottom to cover it evenly. Smooth out the surface with the back of a wet teaspoon.

Bake the cheesecake in the oven for 50 minutes until it's firm to the touch and cream colored, with slightly browned edges. Turn off the heat and open the oven door halfway. Allow the cheesecake to cool slowly in the oven for 1 hour. (If the cake cools too rapidly the top tends to form cracks.) Set the cheesecake aside (in the pan) to chill in the refrigerator for 2 hours.

Release the bottom of the springform pan from its sides. Leave the pan bottom on the cake to keep it from breaking. Carefully peel the parchment paper off the sides of the cake.

Use a long, very sharp knife to cut pieces of cheesecake about 1-inch thick. Press the knife down slowly through the creamy filling, then apply a little more pressure to slice through the crumbly cake bottom. Slide the knife under the slice of cake, between the bottom and the parchment paper, lift, and place each serving on a dessert plate.

The cheesecake keeps for up to 1 week stored in an airtight cake dome in the refrigerator.

ONE SERVING OF CHEESECAKE (ONE SLICE) BAKED KOSHER LIGHT CONTAINS:

 147 CALORIES   3 MGS CHOLESTEROL  0 FAT 95 MGS SODIUM

המנטאשען

HAMANTASCHEN

THESE LEGENDARY PURIM PASTRIES ARE COMMONLY MADE WITH A choice of yeast, shortbread, or biscuit dough. This recipe falls into the crumbly shortbread category, which I prefer. Fresh out of cinnamon, I seasoned it with mace instead, to serendipitous effect. The unusual spice gives this crisp pastry an even crispier flavor, while its exuberant scent pervades the house with celebratory panache.

MAKES EIGHTEEN PASTRIES

2 tablespoons pareve unsalted margarine

⅓ cup plus 2 tablespoons sugar

3 egg whites

½ plus ¼ teaspoon vanilla extract

1 ¼ cups all-purpose flour

2 tablespoons cake flour

1 teaspoon low-sodium baking powder

¼ teaspoon ground mace

¼ teaspoon ground ginger

4 ounces dried apricots (¾ cup)

4 navel orange sections, deveined and seeded (¼ cup)

¾ cup bottled water

½ teaspoon brandy

Canola oil spray

Cut the margarine into ½-inch pieces.

In a food processor or blender, combine the margarine, ⅓ cup of the sugar, the egg whites, and ½ teaspoon of the vanilla extract. Process to blend.

Sift the all-purpose flour, cake flour, baking powder, mace, and ginger together into a medium bowl. Add the flour mixture to the wet ingredients in the food processor or blender. Process to just incorporate. The consistency of the pastry batter is best lumpy. Cover the batter and set it aside in the refrigerator for 2 hours.

To make the fruit filling: Put the apricots, orange sections, the remaining 2 tablespoons of sugar, the remaining ¼ teaspoon of vanilla extract, and the bottled water into a small nonstick saucepan. Bring to a boil.

Lower the heat and cook the fruit mixture at a simmer for 10 to 15 minutes until the fruits begin to break down and the liquid turns thick and syrupy. Set aside to cool for 5 minutes.

Transfer the fruit mixture into a food processor or blender. Add the brandy. Process to just incorporate. The consistency of the hamantaschen filling is best chunky. Yields 2 cups of fruit filling. Cover the filling and set it aside in the refrigerator for 2 hours.

Preheat the oven to 350 degrees.

Quick-spray the bottom of a 14 x 16-inch baking sheet with canola oil. The baking sheet accommodates 9 hamantaschen spaced 1 inch apart. Bake the 18 hamantaschen in 2 batches.

Remove the dough from the refrigerator and put it on a floured board. Spoon out 9 rounded tablespoons of chilled dough. Shape the dough into balls. Flatten the balls of dough into circles 3 inches across and ⅛-inch thick. Place the dough circles on the baking sheet (at this stage they touch).

Remove the fruit filling from the refrigerator. The consistency of the chilled filling is very thick, like preserves. Place 1 rounded teaspoon of filling in the center of each circle of dough. Fold 3 sides of the circles into their centers to make triangular-shaped pastries. The 9 folded pastries are spaced 1 inch apart on the baking sheet.

Bake the pastries in the oven for 30 minutes. The hamantaschen are done when they turn a light golden brown. Set them aside to cool to room temperature. As they cool, the hamantaschen develop a firm, cake-like texture, like shortbread.

Repeat this process with the second batch of 9 hamantaschen.

Hamantaschen keep for weeks stored in an airtight container in the cupboard.

Hamantaschen are pareve.

ONE SERVING OF HAMANTASCHEN (ONE PASTRY) BAKED KOSHER LIGHT CONTAINS:

 58 CALORIES  0 CHOLESTEROL 0 FAT  7 MGS SODIUM

מאן קייק

POPPY SEED CAKE

DON'T BE MISLED BY THE SEEMINGLY INNOCUOUS APPEARANCE

of poppy seeds. Fortunately, a little goes a long way. Those teeny-weeny things are rather high in fat, so there's only enough to ensure a satisfying crunch in every bite. I've further reduced the fat content with nonfat yogurt and the stingiest amount of shortening to keep the batter moist. This cake's airy texture comes from whipping the egg substitute to stand in soft peaks (yes, this can be done!) and gently folding it into the batter.

SERVES EIGHT (MAKES ONE LOAF)

Canola oil spray

2 tablespoons pareve unsalted margarine

¼ container (2 ounces) plain nonfat yogurt (¼ cup)

½ cup sugar

1 ½ teaspoon vanilla extract

1 cup cake flour

1 teaspoon low-sodium baking powder

¼ teaspoon ground nutmeg

2 ounces egg substitute

1 tablespoon poppy seeds

Preheat the oven to 325 degrees.

Quick-spray the bottom and sides of an 8 ½ x 4 ½ x 2 ½-inch loaf pan with canola oil.

Cut the margarine into ½-inch pieces.

In a food processor or blender, combine the margarine, yogurt, sugar, and vanilla extract. Process to blend.

Sift the flour, baking powder, and nutmeg together into a medium bowl.

Add the flour mixture to the wet ingredients in the food processor or blender. Process to blend for 5 minutes until the texture is very smooth and creamy.

Put the egg substitute into a large bowl. Beat until it stands in soft peaks. Fold the creamy flour mixture into the whipped egg substitute with a rubber spatula. The consistency of the cake batter is like whipped cream.

Sprinkle the poppy seeds over all. Stir to distribute the poppy seeds evenly throughout the batter.

Drop the batter into the loaf pan by tablespoons to ensure an airy light texture to the pound cake.

Bake the poppy seed cake in the oven for 30 minutes until it turns ivory colored and lightly browned on the edges. To test for doneness, insert a toothpick into the center of the cake. If it comes out clean, the poppy seed cake is ready. Set the cake aside to cool to room temperature.

Run a knife along the sides of the cake to loosen it from the loaf pan. Invert the pan to release the cake.

Serve the poppy seed cake, sliced 1 inch thick, after a pareve meal of grilled trout or a substantial Israeli salad of chopped tomatoes, cucumbers, and scallions. It's fresh stuff.

Poppy seed cake keeps for up to 5 days in an airtight container in the refrigerator.

SO MUCH FOR YOUR FANCY COOKWARE: In the early days of Israel's statehood, cakes were "baked" on top of the stove in a contraption called the Wonder Pot. The versatile pot had a tightly fitting lid and was made of aluminum or enamel; a funnel inserted in the center gave even heat distribution. Cakes and breads cooked in the Wonder Pot were distinguished by their bundt-like shape. Just as Israelis were savoring their newly won independence, even old-fashioned challah had a delightful ring to it.

ONE SERVING OF POPPY SEED CAKE (ONE SLICE) BAKED KOSHER LIGHT CONTAINS:

 113 CALORIES ♥ 0 CHOLESTEROL  2 GMS FAT ⬛ 14 MGS SODIUM

NOODLE KUGEL

HOW DO YOU RE-CREATE THE CREAMINESS OF OLD-FASHIONED *lokshen* kugel with a modicum of fat? Use nonfat yogurt and part-skim ricotta cheese. There's no sugar added to this recipe. You'll get all the sweetness your palate desires with golden raisins, while the apples, which stay crisp throughout the baking, add a refinement of tartness.

SERVES 8 (MAKES ONE NINE-INCH PUDDING)

Canola oil spray

6 ounces yolk-free egg noodles

1 medium Granny Smith apple

1 teaspoon freshly squeezed lemon juice

2 ounces golden raisins (¼ cup)

3 egg whites

¾ container (6 ounces) nonfat plain yogurt (¾ cup)

¾ container (6 ounces) part-skim ricotta cheese (¾ cup)

2 teaspoons vanilla extract

⅓ cup unsweetened applesauce

½ teaspoon plus ¼ teaspoon ground cinnamon

Preheat the oven to 325 degrees.

Quick-spray the sides and bottom of a 9-inch cake pan with canola oil.

Put 8 cups of water into a medium pot and bring to a boil. Add the noodles by handfuls to keep the water at a rolling boil. Boil the noodles for 8 to 10 minutes to cook them al dente. Drain the noodles and set aside. Yields about 2 ½ cups.

Quick-spray the inside of a medium bowl with canola oil. Put the noodles into the bowl and toss to evenly coat the noodles with oil.

Peel and core the apple. Cut the apple into quarters and chop it into ¼-inch cubes. Drizzle the lemon juice all over to prevent the apple flesh from turning brown.

Into the bowl of noodles, add the apple, raisins, and egg whites. Stir to mix well, distributing the ingredients evenly throughout. Set the noodle and fruit mixture aside.

Put the yogurt, ricotta, vanilla extract, and ¼ teaspoon of the cinnamon into a food processor or blender. Process to blend well. Add the applesauce. Mix to incorporate. The consistency of the cheese mixture is best thick and smooth.

Add the cheese mixture to the noodle and fruit mixture. Stir the kugel batter vigorously to incorporate all of the ingredients.

Pour the batter into the cake pan. Sprinkle the remaining ½ teaspoon of cinnamon over all. Cover the kugel with aluminum foil.

Bake the kugel in the oven for 1 hour until the top turns toasty brown. To test for doneness, insert a toothpick into the center of the kugel. If it comes out clean, the kugel is ready. Set the kugel aside to cool to room temperature.

Use a very sharp knife to slice the kugel into 8 pieces, each 1-inch thick. Serve at room temperature.

Noodle kugel keeps in the refrigerator for up to 5 days stored in an airtight container.

AN EXCHANGE OF YIDDISH INSULTS — IT'S A FOOD FIGHT: Kugel literally means "round" in Yiddish, but in America we know it as "pudding." The word has an another, rather unfortunate definition, too. In England and in South Africa, a kugel is a spoiled Jewish woman (the cousin of a Jewish American Princess). The question is, what do "kugels" call the person who refers to them in this disparaging way? A lox — what else! — they'll have him for lunch on a bagel.

ONE SERVING OF NOODLE KUGEL (ONE SLICE) BAKED KOSHER LIGHT CONTAINS:

 102 CALORIES   ♥ 3 MGS CHOLESTEROL   0 FAT    42 MGS SODIUM

מרבל קייק

MARBLED POUND CAKE

CONVENTIONAL POUND CAKE RECIPES CALL FOR A STICK OF BUTTER and five or more eggs. A slice contains about thirteen grams of fat. We won't even bother with the cholesterol count — it's too depressing. You'd never guess by looking at it, but my marbled pound cake has less than three grams of fat in each powdery slice. Even the ribbon of swirling cocoa is virtually fat-free. The recipe uses two tablespoons of unsalted margarine and, of course, the invaluable egg substitute. That's how it's done!

SERVES EIGHT (MAKES ONE LOAF)

Canola oil spray	1 ½ teaspoons vanilla extract
2 tablespoons pareve unsalted margarine	1 cup cake flour
¼ container (2 ounces) nonfat plain yogurt (¼ cup)	1 teaspoon low-sodium baking powder
	2 ounces egg substitute
½ cup sugar	1 ½ teaspoons unsweetened cocoa powder

Preheat the oven to 325 degrees.

Quick-spray the bottom and sides of an 8 ½ x 4 ½ x 2 ½-inch loaf pan with canola oil.

Cut the margarine into ½-inch pieces.

In a food processor or blender, combine the margarine, yogurt, sugar, and vanilla extract. Process to blend.

Sift the flour and the baking powder together into a medium bowl.

Add the flour mixture to the wet ingredients in the food processor or blender and process to blend for 5 minutes until the texture is very smooth and creamy.

Put the egg substitute into a large bowl. Beat until it stands in soft peaks. Fold the creamy flour mixture into the whipped egg substitute with a rubber spatula. The consistency of the cake batter is like golden whipped cream.

To marble the batter: Pour ½ cup of batter into a medium bowl. Add the cocoa powder. Stir to mix. The chocolate batter is the consistency of thick pudding.

Drop 3 tablespoons of plain batter into the loaf pan. Spread it to evenly cover the bottom of the pan. Drizzle 1 tablespoon of chocolate batter on top. Repeat this process with the remaining batters — alternating plain and chocolate — until all of the batter is used.

Bake the marbled pound cake in the oven for 30 minutes until it turns ivory colored with deep brown swirls of chocolate. To test for doneness, insert a toothpick into the center of the cake. If it comes out clean, the marbled pound cake is ready. Set the cake aside to cool to room temperature.

Run a knife along the sides of the cake to loosen it from the loaf pan. Invert the pan to release the cake.

The marbled pound cake serves 8 — cut the cake into slices about 1-inch thick.

Marbled pound cake keeps for up to 5 days stored in an airtight container in the refrigerator.

FINDING MEANING IN AN EGG: Jewish mystics believed that the egg symbolized both life and death. Raw, it signified the life force — fed to babies as a shield against evil and to brides as fertility food. Eggs roasted in ashes or hard-boiled represented death and mourning. Modern day ceremonies give eggs a place of honor still: hardboiled eggs are eaten on the Ninth of Av, the holiday commemorating the destruction of the Second Temple, and on Passover, a roasted egg is part of the seder plate.

ONE SERVING OF MARBLED POUND CAKE (ONE SLICE) BAKED KOSHER LIGHT CONTAINS:

 108 CALORIES ♥ 0 CHOLESTEROL 2 GMS FAT ☐ 14 MGS SODIUM

פֿליישיג

FLEISHIG (MEAT) DISHES

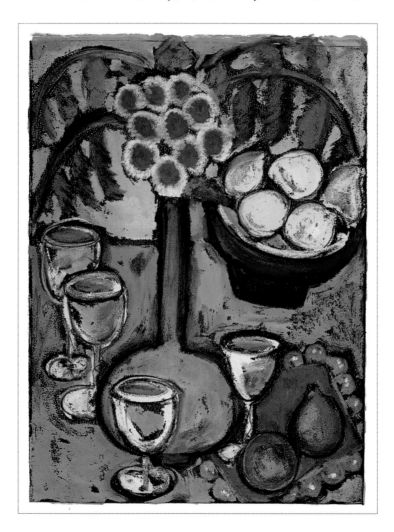

FLEISHIG STARTERS & SIDE DISHES

POTATO KUGEL

PICKLED SALMON

CHICKEN SOUP

MATZAH BALLS (KNAIDLACH)

CHALLAH BREAD

CHOPPED CHICKEN LIVER

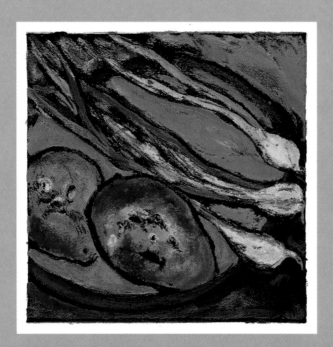

POTATO KUGEL

NO CHICKEN FAT. NO EGG YOLKS. HERBS ARE THE OPERATIVE FLAVORS, egg whites the binding agents in my *Kosher Light* potato kugel. Aromatic rosemary and sage fill the kitchen as nouvelle kugels bake in the oven. Savory mini-puddings prepared in tidy, scrupulously fair muffin cups mean no fussing over who gets the crunchier slice. Potato kugel is a traditional accompaniment for slow-cooked *cholent* or roasted meats. I think, however, it's quite right with scrambled egg whites for your morning eye-opener. In any case, enjoy the nouvelle nosh.

MAKES EIGHT MINI-KUGELS

Canola oil spray

2 medium Idaho potatoes (1 ¼ pounds)

½ cup grated white onion

1 teaspoon pressed garlic

1 tablespoon sodium-free matzah meal

3 egg whites

¼ teaspoon dried sage

¼ teaspoon minced fresh rosemary

Freshly ground black pepper to taste

Preheat the oven to 350 degrees.

Quick-spray the insides of 8 nonstick muffin cups with canola oil. (Each muffin cup is 3 x 1 ¼ inches.)

Scrub the potatoes under cold water. Peel and slice into quarters. Put the slices of potato into a food processor or blender. Coarsely grate to yield 2 cups.

Pour ½ cup of the grated potatoes into a fine-meshed metal sieve. Place the sieve over a small bowl and, using the back of a large spoon, press the water out of the grated potatoes into the bowl. Empty the sieve of dehydrated potatoes into a second bowl. Repeat this process for the remaining grated potatoes.

Set the bowl of potato water aside for 5 minutes to allow the potato starch to sink to the bottom.

Into the bowl of grated potatoes, add the onion, garlic, matzah meal, egg whites, sage, rosemary, and black pepper (to taste). Stir the batter vigorously, distributing the ingredients evenly throughout. The texture of the batter is best lumpy.

Now, turn your attention to the bowl of reserved liquid. Carefully pour off the water to reveal about 1 tablespoon of starch at the bottom of the bowl. Scoop up the starch with a spoon and add it to the kugel batter. Mix to incorporate.

Place ½ cup of kugel batter into each muffin cup.

Bake the little kugels in the oven for 1 hour. The kugels are done when they're brown and crispy on the top and soft and moist in the center.

Run a knife around the sides of each hot little kugel to loosen it from its muffin cup.

Invert the pan to release the kugels.

If you want to serve the mini-kugels before the main course, I like them with refreshing applesauce. As a side dish, they're a perfect partner for stuffed cabbage, soaking up the delicious tomato sauce. Either way, your guests won't be shy — these kugels disappear in the first round.

Potato kugel is pareve and kosher for Passover.

THE SCHMALTZ WAY: In homes throughout the shtetls of Central and Eastern Europe, Jewish families used schmaltz (rendered goose or chicken fat) in many ways, not just for cooking. They swallowed schmaltz to relieve heartburn and used it as a binding agent in cosmetics. They healed their chapped hands with it. Schmaltz was an all-purpose lubricating agent. During the harsh winter, mothers rubbed it on their children's chests to prevent coughs and colds. How times have changed!

ONE SERVING OF POTATO KUGEL (ONE MINI-KUGEL) COOKED KOSHER LIGHT CONTAINS:

49 CALORIES ♥ 0 CHOLESTEROL 0 FAT 18 MGS SODIUM

פֿיקלד לאַקס

PICKLED SALMON

HERE'S A PICKLED FISH TO TICKLE YOU PINK. TANGY PIECES OF TENDER salmon tangled in crunchy onion rings and sprinkled with fiery chili peppers never fails to delight dinner guests. Funny thing, while the preparation is almost effortless, the stream of praise is endless. Pickled salmon is a Jewish standard that is light without conversion. The assertive blend of spices — mustard, fennel, and coriander seeds — gives this particular pickle its lip-smacking flavor. You'll wonder what all the fuss over that frumpy herring was all about.

SERVES FOUR

⅓ cup freshly squeezed lemon juice	¾ teaspoon mustard seeds
2 tablespoons sugar	2 cloves garlic, peeled and flattened
½ cup white wine vinegar	6 dried red chili peppers
½ cup bottled water	2 pods cardamom
½ teaspoon black peppercorns	½ pound salmon fillet, cut into
½ teaspoon fennel seeds	½-inch cubes
½ teaspoon coriander seeds	3 cups thinly sliced onion rings

In a large nonreactive baking pan, combine the lemon juice, sugar, vinegar, water, pepper-corns, fennel seeds, coriander seeds, mustard seeds, garlic, chili peppers, and the car-damom pods. Stir to mix. Set aside for 20 minutes to allow the flavors of the moistened spices to develop.

Add the cubed salmon. Toss to coat. Scatter the onion rings over all to cover. Fill a large serving spoon with marinade from the bottom of the dish and drizzle liquid over the onions. Repeat several times until the onions are well coated. Cover and set aside in the refrigerator to maturate overnight.

Remove the cubes of pickled salmon from the marinade and set them aside.

Put the onion rings and marinade, including the cloves of garlic, chili peppers, and cardamom pods into a large nonstick skillet with a tightly fitting lid. Stir to evenly distribute. Cover the skillet and bring to a boil.

Uncover the skillet and lower the heat to slow the marinade to a bubbling simmer. Add the pickled salmon. Cover the skillet and poach the fish over medium-low heat for 6 minutes. Remove from the heat and set aside to steam for 5 minutes until the salmon is cooked tender. To test for doneness, gently pierce the salmon with a fork. If the fork slides in and out easily, the fish is ready. Set aside to cool to room temperature.

Transfer the pickled salmon, onion rings, and tart poaching liquid into an airtight container and place in the refrigerator to chill for 2 hours.

As a starter salad, pickled salmon (don't forget the piquant onion rings) is simply served on a bed of crispy greens. No need to dress; it comes equipped.

Pickled salmon keeps in the refrigerator for 5 days stored in an airtight container.

Pickled salmon is pareve.

NEW WORLD PICKLE: In the shtetls of Eastern Europe, fresh-caught herring was pickled in oil and vinegar and served with raw onion and boiled potatoes. Pickling to preserve food extended to vegetables, too. Pickled cabbage, beets, and cucumber were staples. When our grandparents emigrated to America, they took stock of the available foods in the New World, including salmon, and incorporated them into their culinary repertoire. Thus, the New York delicacy, pickled salmon was born.

ONE SERVING OF PICKLED SALMON COOKED KOSHER LIGHT CONTAINS:

144 CALORIES   **31** MGS CHOLESTEROL    **4** GMS FAT   **33** MGS SODIUM

טשיקען זופ

CHICKEN SOUP

WHAT'S JEWISH CHICKEN SOUP WITHOUT CHICKEN FAT AND LOTS of salt for flavor? A right turn away from bypass heart surgery — but taste-wise, a tricky proposition. In search of inspiration and healthful stand-in ingredients, I rely on fragrant herbs to preserve the soup's warmth and comfort without sacrificing the familiar stand-up flavor. Combine the pungency of fresh roasted garlic and the piquancy of fresh lemon steeped with the traditional carrot, onion, leek, and parsnip for earthy sweetness. (The veggies are cooked to perfection — as opposed to within an inch of their lives.) A cube of lean beef adds depth and hardiness.

SERVES EIGHT (MAKES EIGHT CUPS)

1 large yellow onion, quartered	2 quarts bottled water
1 large leek, white part only, cut into ½-inch rounds (½ cup)	6 medium carrots, peeled and cut into ½-inch rounds (3 cups)
2 pounds chicken backs and necks	1 medium parsnip, peeled and cut into ½-inch rounds (½ cup)
¼ ounce chuck steak	
1 large lemon, seeded and quartered	1 medium head garlic
Pinch black peppercorns	8 pieces (5-inch square) cheese cloth
½ bunch fresh dill, snipped (¼ cup)	Cayenne pepper to taste

In a large heavy-bottomed pot with a tightly fitting lid, or a 5-quart Dutch oven, combine the onion, leek, chicken, steak, lemon, peppercorns, and half the dill. Add the water and bring to a boil. Lower the heat and simmer the broth for 30 minutes.

Add the carrots and parsnip and cook at a simmer for 30 minutes more until tender.

Remove the pot from the heat and set it aside to cool to room temperature.

Strain the broth through a colander into a large bowl. Set the bowl of broth aside in the refrigerator for 3 to 4 hours until a hard layer of chicken fat forms on the surface.

Reserve all the strained ingredients, except the onion, lemon, and the peppercorns. Skin and bone the chicken parts to yield about ½ cup of slivered chicken. Dice the steak cube. Combine the slivered chicken and diced steak with the carrot, parsnip, and leek. Place the mixture into an airtight container and set aside in the refrigerator.

To make the roasted garlic: Preheat the oven to 350 degrees.

Put the head of garlic into a small baking pan. Bake it in the oven for 1 hour. The garlic is done when the outside is golden brown and the papery skin yields to a gentle poke. Set aside to cool to room temperature.

Separate the head into individual cloves. To remove the roasted garlic meat, squeeze the tip of the clove to push the softened garlic out the opposite end of its shell. Repeat this process for each clove to yield

about 3 tablespoons of roasted garlic. Set aside.

Wash the soup pot or Dutch oven in preparation for reheating the broth.

Carefully remove the hardened layer of chicken fat on the surface of the cold broth. Use a spatula to lift the fat in one piece, if possible, or several large pieces. Collect any small fragments of hardened fat with the tip of a spoon or the point of a knife until the broth is virtually fat free.

Line the bottom and sides of a fine-meshed metal sieve with the layers of cheese cloth. Strain the broth into the clean soup pot.

Cover the pot and bring the chicken soup to a boil. Lower the heat and add the roasted garlic and the reserved chicken and vegetable mixture. Stir. Season with cayenne pepper (to taste). Sprinkle the remaining snipped dill over all. Stir. Cover the pot and simmer for 10 to 15 minutes until the chicken soup is piping hot. Transfer the soup to a tureen.

Before serving, give the chicken soup a stir so that each portion contains scrumptious bites of vegetables and chicken.

Chicken soup keeps in the refrigerator for

up to 5 days, stored in an airtight container.

Although the *Kosher Light* chicken soup recipe doesn't produce a clear broth, it's light, fat-free, and flavorful, making it a delicious liquid base (as I suggest) for stuffed cabbage, beef *cholent*, and chicken matzah pie.

Freeze several cups of the chicken soup in individual ice cube molds to use on the spur of the moment to enhance your other fleishig favorites. The roasted-garlic flavor adds mellow warmth to stews, soups, dips, and sauces. Frozen in this way, the chicken soup keeps indefinitely.

WHY WOULD ASHKENAZIM OF YORE BE AGHAST AT A SALAD BAR? *Jewish food historian Oded Schwartz explains it this way: In general, Jews from the old country had an aversion to uncooked food. (They considered anything raw to be bloody, pagan, and forbidden.) In particular, they'd have nothing to do with uncooked vegetables, except for raw onion, garlic, and radish. The saying "melts in your mouth" may be traced to this preference for foods cooked soft and served piping hot.*

ONE SERVING OF CHICKEN SOUP (ONE CUP) COOKED KOSHER LIGHT CONTAINS:

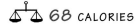 68 CALORIES   ♥ 13MGS CHOLESTEROL   0 FAT    25MGS SODIUM

MATZAH BALLS (KNAIDLACH)

THIS RECIPE PRODUCES DAINTY LITTLE KNAIDLACH. BUT DON'T worry — there's plenty to go around. The matzah balls are scented with garlic, dill, and a nip of cayenne, so there's no need for salt. As for the (in)famous dumpling debate, arguing the merits of sinkers vs. floaters, I've taken the light way — no dense dumplings here. The tasty morsels are firm to fork, but tender to tooth.

MAKES TWENTY-FOUR MINI MATZAH BALLS

1 tablespoon pareve unsalted margarine

2 tablespoons slivered garlic

2 tablespoons freshly squeezed lemon juice

2 tablespoons bottled water

½ cup plus 2 tablespoons sodium-free matzah meal

4 ounces egg substitute

2 tablespoons snipped fresh dill

Freshly ground black pepper to taste

Cayenne pepper to taste

In a small saucepan over medium heat, melt the margarine. Add the garlic. Sauté for 2 minutes until the garlic starts to soften. Add 1 tablespoon of the lemon juice. Lower the heat and continue to sauté for 2 minutes more, stirring, until the garlic begins to turn golden.

Transfer the sautéed garlic and its cooking liquid into a large bowl. Add the bottled water and stir. Add the matzah meal and mix to moisten evenly. Add the egg substitute and stir to combine. Add the snipped dill and stir to incorporate. Sprinkle over all with the black pepper and cayenne pepper (to taste). Stir the mixture thoroughly — the batter is the consistency of cooked cream of wheat. Yields 1 ¼ cups. Cover and set aside to chill in the refrigerator for 15 minutes.

Put 6 cups of water and the remaining 1 tablespoon of lemon juice into a large, heavy-bottomed pot with a tightly fitting lid, or a 5-quart Dutch oven. Cover and bring to a boil. Uncover, lower the heat to medium-high, and bring the lemony water to a bubbling simmer.

Spoon out 1 teaspoon of chilled batter and shape it into a ball about 1 inch across. Drop the matzah dumpling into the simmering water. Repeat this process for the remaining batter to yield 24 small dumplings.

Cover the pot and cook at a bubbling simmer for 30 minutes until the dumplings expand slightly and bob to the surface. To test for doneness, insert a toothpick into the center of one. If it comes out clean, the knaidlach are ready.

Lift the matzah balls out of the water with a slotted spoon and set them aside on a large platter to cool to room temperature.

If you're preparing the knaidlach ahead of time, they keep for 3 days in an airtight container in the refrigerator. The matzah balls are best reheated in simmering soup.

Otherwise they're good to go, served 4 to a customer, floating proudly in bowls of piping hot homemade soup.

Matzah balls are pareve.

A GIFT FROM THE PEASANTS: Matzah balls are the kosher-for-Passover version of dumplings, an essential peasant food of Central Europe since Medieval times. Inventive serfs boiled dollops of bread crumbs moistened with eggs in their meager stew pots and the dumpling was born out of necessity. Their Jewish neighbors adapted the recipe by adding crushed matzah and chicken fat to the batter. Virtually unchanged for six hundred years, the modern matzah ball is still seasoned with onions and parsley.

ONE SERVING OF MATZAH BALLS (FOUR BABY DUMPLINGS) COOKED KOSHER LIGHT CONTAINS:

83 CALORIES ♥ *0* CHOLESTEROL *0* FAT *29* MGS SODIUM

CHALLAH BREAD

HOW DO YOU REPRODUCE THE RICH TASTE OF CHALLAH WITHOUT

egg yolks? For assistance with this challenge, I turned to Mike Rose, co-owner of Semifreddi's kosher bakery in Emeryville, California. He recommended sweet potato to moisten the dough and reproduce the soft yellow color of challah made with real eggs, not substitute. The taste of sweet potato is quite mild, so it won't intrude on the challah flavor. This recipe produces loaves with a wonderfully tender and thready texture, the distinguishing features of the bread of Shabbat.

MAKES TWO LOAVES OF CHALLAH

1 medium sweet potato (¾ pound)	4 ounces egg substitute
3 tablespoons pareve unsalted margarine	5 ¾ cups plus ¼ cup flour
2 packages active dry yeast	Canola oil spray
⅓ cup plus ¼ teaspoon bottled water	1 sheet (14 x 16-inch) parchment paper
2 tablespoons honey	1 egg white

Scrub the sweet potato under cold water. Peel and slice into quarters.

In a medium pot with a tightly fitting lid, bring 4 cups of water to a boil. Add the sweet potato and cook at a boil for 15 to 20 minutes until the sweet potato is soft and cooked through. Transfer the sweet potato to a large plate and set it aside to cool to room temperature.

Cut the margarine into ½-inch pieces.

Mash the sweet potato and set it aside. Yields 1 ¼ cups.

Combine the margarine, yeast, mashed sweet potato, the ⅓ cup of water, the honey, and egg substitute in a food processor or blender. Process to blend.

Put the 5 ¾ cups of flour into a large bowl.

Add the wet ingredients to the bowl of flour. Mix the batter with a large wooden spoon to distribute the ingredients evenly throughout. The consistency of the challah batter is best lumpy.

On a floured board, knead the batter until it turns into a smooth, highly elastic, and slightly sticky dough. Add the remaining ¼ cup of flour 1 teaspoon at a time until the dough ceases to be sticky. Don't over-knead — challah dough is best pliable and elastic. Roll the dough into a ball.

Quick-spray the inside of a large bowl with canola oil. Place the dough ball in the bowl and turn the dough to coat it well with oil. Cover the bowl with a towel and set it aside in a warm place for 1 hour.

Remove the towel and re-cover the bowl with plastic wrap. Set it aside in the refrigerator to chill overnight.

Discard the plastic wrap and re-cover the ball of dough with a towel. Set it aside in a warm place for 1 hour until it returns to room temperature.

Knead the dough ball to eliminate bubbles. Divide the dough in half (each half to become a loaf of bread). Cover the dough halves with a towel and set them aside to rest for 5 minutes.

Divide one dough half into 3 equal pieces. Roll each piece into a 1-foot-long rope or snake shape. Pinch the ropes at one end to attach them to each other and braid them together. Pinch the bottom of the braid closed. Neatly tuck the braid tips under the loaf at either end to create the football-like shape of a classic challah. Repeat this process to shape the second challah bread.

Line a 14 x 16-inch baking sheet with parchment paper.

Place the challahs 3 inches apart on the baking sheet. Cover with a towel. Set the loaves aside in a warm spot for 45 minutes until they almost double in size and spring back immediately when dented with the tip of your finger.

Preheat the oven to 375 degrees.

Put the remaining ¼ teaspoon of water

and egg white into a small bowl. Mix to combine. Using a basting brush, paint the tops and sides of the loaves with the egg white mixture to glaze. (Our bubbies used chicken feathers!)

Bake the loaves in the oven for 30 minutes until the challahs are 1 foot long and turn a shiny medium brown all over. To test for doneness, tap the crust with your knuckles.

If you get a hollow sound, it's time to take the challahs out of the oven.

Serve toasted challah with scrambled egg whites for a kosher light breakfast. Challah makes super French toast, too.

The loaves of challah keep for up to 2 weeks stored in the freezer, tightly wrapped in aluminum foil.

Challah bread is pareve.

HOLY CHALLAH: In biblical times, it was a pious deed (a mitzvah) to give the temple priests an offering of a small piece of dough torn from the Sabbath bread. Commemorating this ancient ritual ("to separate challah"), observant Jewish women pinch off an olive-sized piece of dough from their Sabbath challah just before the loaf goes into the oven. Then they recite a prayer to sanctify the divine command of separating the challah. Afterwards, they burn the piece of dough over an open flame.

ONE SERVING OF CHALLAH BREAD (ONE SLICE) BAKED KOSHER LIGHT CONTAINS:

 98 CALORIES   0 CHOLESTEROL   1 GM FAT   9 MGS SODIUM

טשאפּד לעבער

CHOPPED CHICKEN LIVER

LAST TIME MY BROTHER RON THE JEWISH DOCTOR WATCHED ME devour a chopped liver sandwich, he nearly had a stroke. "Cholesterol, cholesterol, cholesterol," he murmured over his egg white omelet. There's no arguing with the doc on that score. What to do, since I want my chopped liver and my health too? The solution: a *Kosher Light* version made with only enough chicken liver for a good flavor (two ounces, to be exact), combined with plump brown mushrooms, lots of onion, tasty shallots, and tangy roasted garlic. Compare the difference: A quarter-cup of the traditionally prepared kind weighs in at over 300 mg of cholesterol and who knows how many grams of fat? My recipe contains 58 mgs of cholesterol and less than one gram of fat per serving. Go for it, maybe not totally guilt-free, but where's the fun in that?

SERVES SIX

2 whole chicken livers (2 ounces), cut in half	¼ cup chopped shallots
½ teaspoon kosher salt	2 tablespoons Madeira wine
Olive oil spray	2 tablespoons Roasted Garlic (*page 56*)
¾ pound brown mushrooms, thinly sliced (3 cups)	½ cup minced yellow onion
	1 hard-boiled egg white, chopped
½ teaspoon minced fresh rosemary	Freshly ground black pepper to taste
Pinch ground nutmeg	1 sprig fresh parsley for garnish

To prepare the chicken livers according to the *Laws of Kashrut:* Remove the broiling tray from the oven. Cover it with aluminum foil.

Preheat the broiler.

Using a sharp knife, lightly score the chicken livers on both sides. Rinse them under cold water. Sprinkle them evenly all over with kosher salt.

Arrange the chicken livers on the broiling tray. Broil for 2 to 3 minutes. Turn the livers over and cook for 2 minutes more. The livers are done when the insides turn a light-brown color without a trace of pink. The delicate livers cook very quickly. In order to prepare them strictly kosher they must be cooked through completely; however, don't let them get well done or the chopped liver comes out dry and dense.

Rinse the broiled livers under cold water to wash off the salt and the cooking juices. Pat dry and set aside.

Quick-spray the bottom of a medium nonstick skillet with olive oil. Add the mushrooms, rosemary, nutmeg, and shallots. Sauté over medium heat for 1 or 2 minutes to wilt the mushrooms. Drizzle the Madeira wine over all. Sauté for about 5 minutes more until the mushrooms soften.

Transfer the mushroom mixture and its juices into a food processor or blender. Add the chicken livers, roasted garlic, onion, and egg white. Process to blend. Add the black pepper (to taste). Continue to pulse-blend until the chopped liver is the texture of a smooth country-style pâté. Yields 1 ½ cups.

Spoon the chopped chicken liver into a serving bowl. With the flat edge of a metal spatula, swirl the top of the liver to give the surface a finished presentation. Garnish with a fresh parsley sprig.

Your preference: Serve at room temperature or lightly chilled. Any way, nothing's better than chopped chicken liver spread on bite-sized pieces of (sodium-free!) matzah.

ONE SERVING OF CHOPPED CHICKEN LIVER (ONE-QUARTER CUP) COOKED KOSHER LIGHT CONTAINS:

49 CALORIES   58 MGS CHOLESTEROL   0 FAT   16 MGS SODIUM

FLEISHIG MAIN COURSES

STUFFED CABBAGE

BEEF CHOLENT

CHICKEN MATZAH PIE

BRISKET TZIMMES

CHICKEN FRICASSEE

סטעפר קאבעג

STUFFED CABBAGE

STUFFED CABBAGE IS THE MOST FUN OF ALL THE CLASSIC JEWISH
recipes to prepare. My *Kosher Light* adaptation substitutes lean and light ground turkey for
the traditional filling of ground beef. A finishing touch of tart fresh lemon juice boosts the
tomatoey taste of the sweet-and-sour sauce.

MAKES EIGHT STUFFED CABBAGE ROLLS

1 medium cabbage	Freshly ground black pepper to taste
1 ½ cans (14 ½ ounces each) low-sodium tomato puree (2 ⅔ cups)	Cayenne pepper to taste
	Olive oil spray
½ cup bottled water	1 ½ cups minced onion
2 tablespoons packed brown sugar	½ teaspoon minced fresh rosemary
1 ½ ounces golden raisins (¼ cup)	4 ounces arborio rice (½ cup)
3 tablespoons dry red wine	½ cup Chicken Soup (*page 55*)
1 teaspoon pressed garlic	1 pound ground turkey
¼ plus ¼ teaspoon dried thyme	1 small lemon, quartered for garnish

Rinse the cabbage under cold water. Pat dry. Core the cabbage.

Put 8 cups of water into a large, heavy-bottomed pot with a tightly fitting lid, or a 5-quart Dutch oven. Bring to a boil. Lower the heat and add the cored cabbage. Cover and cook at a simmer for 10 minutes until the cabbage leaves wilt.

Transfer the cabbage to a colander to drain. Set it aside to cool to room temperature.

Combine the tomato puree, the bottled water, brown sugar, raisins, wine, garlic, and ¼ teaspoon of the thyme in a medium bowl. Sprinkle the black pepper and cayenne pepper over all (to taste). Stir to combine the ingredients thoroughly. Yields about 3 ⅓ cups of tomato sauce. Set aside.

Quick-spray the bottom of a medium nonstick skillet with olive oil. Add the onion, the remaining ¼ teaspoon of thyme, and the rosemary. Sauté over medium heat for 4 or 5 minutes until the onion turns soft. Add the rice and stir to coat. Add the chicken soup and sauté for 5 minutes more until the rice absorbs all the liquid.

Transfer the rice into a medium bowl. Add the turkey and ¼ cup of the tomato sauce. Stir to mix the turkey stuffing thoroughly.

Now, turn your attention to the parcooked head of cabbage. Remove 8 medium-sized leaves from the head of cabbage. Place 4 tablespoons of turkey stuffing just below the center of a cabbage leaf. Fold the leaf in half to cover the filling and to form a half-moon-shaped package. Fold the sides into the center of the package. Starting at the filled end, roll up the stuffed cabbage to form a cylinder about 3 inches long. Repeat this process for the remaining 7 leaves.

Preheat the oven to 300 degrees.

Into a 13 x 9-inch baking pan with a tightly fitting lid, pour ¾ cup of tomato sauce. Spread the sauce to evenly cover the bottom of the pan. Add the cabbage rolls, seam-side down, and ¼ inch apart. Pour the remaining 2 ⅓ cups of tomato sauce over all. Cover the baking pan.

Bake the stuffed cabbage rolls in the oven for 2 hours.

Raise the oven temperature to 350 degrees and baste the cabbage rolls with the tangy tomato sauce. Remove the cover and continue to bake for 30 minutes more. The stuffed cabbage rolls are done when the edges are lightly browned.

Serve succulent stuffed cabbage rolls and crisp mini potato kugels together, naturally. Don't forget the garnish — a healthy squeeze of fresh lemon juice brightens the flavor with a zesty finish.

ONE SERVING OF STUFFED CABBAGE (ONE STUFFED CABBAGE ROLL) COOKED KOSHER LIGHT CONTAINS:

 201 CALORIES   29 MGS CHOLESTEROL    6 GMS FAT    60 MGS SODIUM

BEEF CHOLENT

WHEN OUR BUBBIES WERE YOUNG GIRLS, THIS JEWISH PEASANT STEW required slow, overnight cooking to soften the fatty meats that served as the centerpiece of this old-fashioned dish. *Cholent cooked Kosher Light*, using lean chuck steak, creamy barley, hardy beans, and loads more vegetables, still tastes the way you like it. Lean (and less) meat cuts the cholesterol, and parcooked beans cut the cooking time to the better part of a lazy Sunday afternoon. Beef cholent is a one-course, one-bowl dinner to enjoy on its own.

SERVES TWELVE

4 ounces dried Great Northern beans (½ cup)

Olive oil spray

1 ½ cups coarsely chopped yellow onions

2 stalks celery, coarsely chopped (1 cup)

1 tablespoon minced garlic

¾ pound lean chuck steak, cut into cubes

4 ounces dried pearl barley (½ cup)

6 cups Chicken Soup (*page 55*)

3 bay leaves

2 teaspoons paprika

Freshly ground black pepper to taste

8 new red potatoes, cut in half (2 ½ cups)

8 baby carrots, peeled and julienne-sliced (2 cups)

4 sprigs fresh dill for garnish

1 small lemon, quartered for garnish

Put the dried Great Northern beans into a medium pot with a tightly fitting lid. Add enough cold water to cover the beans. Bring to a boil and cook for 2 minutes. Remove from the heat, cover, and set aside for 1 hour. Drain the beans to yield ¾ cup. Discard the bean water. Place the parcooked beans into a bowl and set aside.

Quick-spray the bottom of a large, heavy-bottomed nonstick pot with a tightly fitting lid, or a 5-quart Dutch oven with olive oil. Add the onion, celery, and garlic. Sauté over a low heat for about 5 minutes until the onions turn translucent and the celery softens. Remove the vegetable mixture from the pot and set aside.

Place the steak cubes into the pot. Raise the heat to medium-high and, stirring, sear the meat on all sides for 2 to 3 minutes until it lightly browns.

Turn the heat to low. Return the vegetable mixture to the pot. Stir to evenly distribute. Add the beans and the barley. Toss to mix well. Add 4 cups of the chicken soup to cover. Add the bay leaves. Sprinkle the paprika and the black pepper over all (to taste). Stir. Raise the heat to medium-high and bring the mixture to a boil.

Turn the heat to low and cover the pot. Cook the *cholent* at a slow simmer for 2 hours, stirring occasionally. As the beans and the barley cook they absorb the liquid. Add chicken soup, ½ cup at a time, as needed, to moisten the *cholent* and keep it

from sticking to the bottom of the pot.

Add the potatoes and carrots. Stir in any remaining chicken soup. Continue to cook at a slow simmer, stirring frequently, for 30 minutes until the carrots are tender. The *cholent* is done when the beans are soft and a fork slides easily in and out of the meat and potatoes.

Garnish each steaming-hot bowlful of *cholent* with a sprig of fresh dill and a wedge of lemon.

For dessert, offer chilled baked apples — they're a cool and light counterpoint.

Beef *cholent* keeps in the refrigerator for up to 3 days stored in an airtight container.

ONE SERVING OF BEEF CHOLENT COOKED KOSHER LIGHT CONTAINS:

 187 CALORIES    35 MGS CHOLESTEROL    2 GMS FAT    41 MGS SODIUM

טשיקען מצה פאי

CHICKEN MATZAH PIE

EGYPTIAN JEWS CALL THE DISH MAYEENA. THE JEWISH MOROCCANS'
name for it is *pastilla*, or *bastila*. My cousins in Haifa refer to it as *pashtidah*. The Ladino
term is *mina de Pesach*. This classic Sephardic savory pastry came about because of the
need to use the leftover chicken or turkey from the Pesach seder. My *Kosher Light* pie is filled
with sautéed mushrooms, seasoned with sage and tarragon. The quantity of roasted
chicken is virtually in name only — the flavorful torte hardly needs the meat to qualify as a
candidate for your personal Jewish comfort food canon. This one's a shoo-in.

SERVES EIGHT

Olive oil spray

1 ½ cups coarsely chopped yellow onion

1 tablespoon minced garlic

¾ pound white mushrooms, sliced (3 cups)

1 medium carrot, peeled and julienne-sliced (½ cup)

1 teaspoon dried tarragon

½ teaspoon dried sage

¼ teaspoon cayenne pepper

Pinch saffron

1 roasted chicken thigh, skinned and shredded (1 cup)

1 teaspoon Madeira wine

3 ½ ounces egg substitute

Freshly ground black pepper to taste

6 sodium-free matzahs

1 cup Chicken Soup (*page 55*)

Preheat the oven to 350 degrees.

Quick-spray the bottom of a large nonstick skillet with olive oil. Add the chopped onion,
minced garlic, mushrooms, carrot, tarragon, sage, cayenne, and saffron. Sauté over low heat
for 5 minutes until the onions turn translucent and the mushrooms soften. Remove the

skillet from the heat and set aside to cool to room temperature.

Transfer the vegetable mixture into a bowl. Add the shredded chicken and the Madeira wine. Toss to combine. Add 2 ½ ounces of egg substitute and mix well to coat evenly. Season with black pepper (to taste). Set the pie filling aside.

Place the matzahs into a large glass or ceramic baking dish. Pour the chicken soup over all to cover. Set aside to soak for 5 minutes until the matzahs are soft and flexible. Carefully transfer the softened matzahs to a large plate.

Add the remaining 1 ounce of egg substitute to the chicken soup in the baking dish. Whisk to combine. Set the mixture aside to use to glaze the top of the chicken matzah pie.

Quick-spray the bottom of an 11 x 7-inch nonstick baking pan with olive oil. Place 2 softened matzahs in the bottom of the baking pan, overlapping the matzahs in the middle. Evenly spread half the filling over the matzahs. Place 2 softened matzahs on top. Evenly spread the remaining pie filling over the second layer of matzahs. Place the last 2 pieces of softened matzah on top of the filling to crown the pie. Drizzle the egg substitute mixture evenly over all to glaze the pie.

Place the matzah pie into the oven and bake for 20 minutes. Quick-spritz the top with olive oil spray and bake for 10 minutes more. The chicken matzah pie is done when the top turns golden brown. Set the pie aside until it's cool enough to handle.

Cutting through the brittle layers of flaky torte requires a bit of finesse. Use a long, very sharp knife to slice the pie into 8 equal portions, each about 1 ½-inches thick.

Serve warm or at room temperature.

בריזקעט צימעס

BRISKET TZIMMES

PUMPKIN GIVES MY TZIMMES A NUTTY FLAVOR AND AN AUTUMNAL
presentation — a holiday touch, honoring the festival of Sukkot. This sweet and savory dish
is seasoned with prunes, golden raisins, and Madeira wine, and spiced the Sephardic way with
cloves, cardamom, ginger, and cinnamon. To keep kosher light, ask the butcher to trim away
the layer of fat that covers the top of the brisket. Not to worry; the meat cooks moist and
flavorful. Naturally, the condiment of choice is white horseradish.

SERVES EIGHT

1 pumpkin (2 ½ pounds), seeded and cut into 3-inch pieces

1 tablespoon honey

Olive oil spray

1 cup coarsely chopped yellow onion

2 teaspoons pressed garlic

¼ teaspoon ground cloves

½ teaspoon ground cinnamon

¼ teaspoon cardamom seeds, crushed

2 teaspoons minced fresh ginger

Pinch cayenne pepper

1 pound first-cut brisket, trimmed of fat

3 ½ ounces pitted prunes, sliced in half (½ cup)

1 ounce golden raisins (⅛ cup)

1 teaspoon torn fresh tarragon

1 tablespoon Madeira wine

Freshly ground black pepper to taste

¼ cup White Horseradish (page 9)

Bring 12 cups of water to a boil in a large stockpot.

Put the pumpkin pieces into the boiling water and cook for 8 minutes. Remove the parcooked
pumpkin and set it aside to cool to room temperature. Reserve 1 cup of pumpkin water.

Combine the pumpkin water and honey in a small bowl. Stir to completely dissolve the honey.

Set the sweetened pumpkin water aside.

Peel the pumpkin pieces and set them aside. Yields 4 cups of skinless pumpkin.

Quick-spray the bottom of a large, heavy-bottomed nonstick pot with a tightly fitting lid, or a 5-quart Dutch oven with olive oil. Add the chopped onion, minced garlic, clove, cardamom, minced ginger, and cayenne pepper. Sauté over low heat for about 5 minutes until the onions turn translucent. Remove the onion mixture from the pot and set aside.

Put the brisket into the pot. Raise the heat to medium-high and sear for 2 to 3 minutes until lightly browned on all sides.

Turn the heat to low and return the onion mixture to the pot. Add the prunes and half the golden raisins. Stir to mix well. Cover the pot and simmer for 1 hour over very low heat to slowly cook the brisket and fruit. After 20 minutes, stir the fruit mixture and baste the meat with the cooking juices. The brisket is done when a fork slides easily in and out of the center. Transfer the brisket to a warmed serving platter. Cover and set aside.

Put the pumpkin into the pot. Add the remaining raisins, the tarragon, Madeira wine, ½ cup of pumpkin water, and black pepper (to taste). Stir to coat the pumpkin with the spicy fruit and cooking juices. Cover and simmer the tzimmes over low heat for 30 minutes, stirring occasionally. Add the remaining sweetened pumpkin water, as needed, to moisten the tzimmes.

Turn off the heat and allow the tzimmes to sit covered for 30 minutes. The tzimmes is done when the pumpkin and fruit are tender. Transfer the tzimmes to a warmed serving bowl.

Use a sharp carving knife to slice the brisket lengthwise with the grain into ¼-inch-thick strips.

Serve several slices of brisket beside a fruit-laden mound of pumpkin tzimmes and 1 or 2 teaspoons of white horseradish. A garnish of crisp parsley is a crown of Sukkot greenery.

Brisket tzimmes keeps for up to 3 days in an airtight container in the refrigerator.

ONE SERVING OF BRISKET TZIMMES COOKED KOSHER LIGHT CONTAINS:

 170 CALORIES   54 MGS CHOLESTEROL    4 GMS FAT   38 MGS SODIUM

פריקעזי

CHICKEN FRICASSEE

IN NEW YORK, CHICKEN FRICASSEE IS AS JEWISH AS CHICKEN SOUP
with matzah balls (I've learned). Having grown up in Nebraska and settled in California, I might
never have taken a fricassee of any kind for Jewish, but for a friend from the old country
(Manhattan), who was shocked by my ignorance. (*You've never heard of chicken fricassee?*) In
order to cook light what is essentially a simple skillet stew, I substituted small broiler
chicken breasts with the skin and fat removed for the flavorful, but fatty and large whole
stewing chickens used in traditional Jewish chicken fricassee. Every gram of sodium counts,
so oil-cured olives in place of the common pickled variety balance the scale. Guided by my
New York friend, the *Kosher Light* version is in all other ways "authentic," with lots of garlic,
paprika, and the other hot-and-spicy things that give this dish its wised-up tang.

SERVES SIX

4 broiler chicken breast halves (2 pounds)	1 jar (2 ounces) pimientos, drained and julienne-sliced
Olive oil spray	
1 cup coarsely chopped yellow onion	8 oil-cured black olives, pitted and chopped
1 large green bell pepper, seeded and julienne-sliced (1 cup)	2 teaspoons balsamic vinegar
	2 sprigs fresh rosemary
3 tablespoons minced garlic	2 tablespoons paprika
1 teaspoon red pepper flakes	Freshly ground black pepper to taste
	Optional: rice, orzo, or yolk-free broad egg noodles for accompaniment

Remove the skin and cut away all of the visible fat from the chicken breasts. Rinse them
under cold water and pat dry. Set aside.

Quick-spray the bottom of a large non-stick skillet with a tightly fitting lid with olive oil. Add the chopped onion, sliced bell pepper, minced garlic, and red pepper flakes. Sauté over low heat for about 5 minutes until the onions turn translucent and the bell peppers soften. Remove the vegetable mixture from the skillet and set aside.

Place the chicken breasts in the skillet. Raise the heat to medium and cook, turning the chicken breasts frequently, for 2 to 3 minutes until lightly brown on all sides.

Lower the heat and return the vegetable mixture to the skillet. Spread it evenly over the chicken breasts. Add the sliced pimiento, chopped olives, and balsamic vinegar. Toss to coat the chicken breasts and distribute the ingredients evenly. Add the rosemary sprigs. Sprinkle the paprika and black pepper (to taste) over all.

Cover the skillet and cook for 10 to 15 minutes over very low heat to slowly simmer the chicken fricassee. Stir and baste once or twice with the simmering cooking juices.

The fricassee is done when a fork slides easily in and out of the meat.

While the chicken fricassee is cooking, prepare rice, orzo, or yolk-free broad egg noodles. Any one of these options serves the fricassee deliciously. About 5 minutes before the fricassee is done cooking, add your choice to the skillet. Toss to coat with the cooking juices and to mix the chicken and vegetables with the rice, orzo, or noodle accompaniment. (If none of these are to your liking, corn or mashed yams team tastily with the fricassee, too — cooked separately, of course, and served on the side.)

Chicken fricassee is best presented family-style on a warmed serving platter — let all who are hungry serve themselves.

ONE SERVING OF CHICKEN FRICASSEE COOKED KOSHER LIGHT CONTAINS:

 **266** CALORIES **116** MGS CHOLESTEROL **5** GMS FAT **100** MGS SODIUM

FLEISHIG DESSERTS

FRUIT COMPOTE

RICE PUDDING

HONEY CAKE (LEKACH)

MATZAH KUGEL

MANDELBROIT

פרוכטן קאמפט

FRUIT COMPOTE

MY FAVORITE DRIED FRUITS — MISSION FIGS, APRICOTS, CHERRIES, and raisins — make so sweet and tangy a combination, they need only rehydrate in citrus-enhanced Madeira to reach the peak of perfection. A super-tart Granny Smith apple adds texture and freshness to the mix; juicy orange sections add a refreshing finishing touch. Fruit compote is a versatile pareve dessert to pair with milchig or fleishig entrees. Is it a Jewish tradition? In my childhood home it was. So long as I can remember, my mother always had a container of fruit compote on hand for Pesach and the High Holy Days.

SERVES EIGHT

¼ cup Madeira wine

1 cup freshly squeezed orange juice

2 tablespoons honey

¼ teaspoon ground cinnamon

⅛ teaspoon ground cardamom

½ teaspoon ground ginger

2 ½ ounces dried mission figs (½ cup)

2 ½ ounces dried apricots (½ cup)

2 ½ ounces dried cherries (½ cup)

3 ounces raisins (½ cup)

1 large Granny Smith apple

3 tablespoons freshly squeezed lemon juice

1 cup bottled water

1 large seedless navel orange

In a large bowl, combine the Madeira wine, orange juice, and 1 tablespoon of the honey. Stir until the honey is completely dissolved. Add the spices: cinnamon, cardamom, and ginger. Stir to incorporate. Add the dried fruit: figs, apricots, cherries, and raisins. Toss to coat well. Cover and set aside to rehydrate for 1 hour, tossing the fruit once more after 30 minutes. Transfer the rehydrated fruit into a small bowl. Reserve the rehydrating liquid.

Peel and core the apple. Cut into quarters and slice the quarters into ½-inch pieces. Drizzle 1 tablespoon of the lemon juice over all to prevent the apple flesh from turning brown. Set aside.

Peel, devein, and divide the orange into sections. Set aside.

Combine the remaining lemon juice, the remaining 1 tablespoon honey, the rehydrating liquid, and the bottled water in a medium nonstick pot with a tightly fitting lid. Stir to mix well. Cover and bring to a boil.

Uncover the pot and lower the heat to medium to slow the sweetened water to a simmer. Add the figs, apricots, cherries, and raisins. Cover the pot and cook at a simmer for 10 minutes. Add the sliced apple. Cover and cook for 5 minutes more. The fruit compote is done when the apples are just tender. Yields 8 cups. Set aside to cool to room temperature.

If you're serving the fruit compote on the day of preparation, transfer the compote, including its delicious juices, to a serving bowl. Arrange the orange slices on top.

Cover and chill in the refrigerator for 1 hour.

If you're preparing the fruit compote ahead of time, garnish with the orange slices and place it in an airtight container in the refrigerator. The dessert keeps indefinitely stored in this way. In fact, the orange slices become especially succulent over time as they drink in the ruby-red juice and wine.

Fruit compote is pareve.

THAT FIG WAS SOME TOMATO: In Middle Eastern mythology, a fig was the symbol for femininity and motherhood. Biblical writings linked the fig to female sexuality and fertility. In archaic Hebrew, the word "paga" (an unripe fig) was also used to describe a preadolescent girl. The Biblical phrase, "the time when the fig begins to ripen," referred to coming of age sexually; the image of a fruitless fig tree was a metaphor for barrenness. So . . . be fruitful and multiply!

ONE SERVING OF FRUIT COMPOTE (ONE CUP) COOKED KOSHER LIGHT CONTAINS:

111 CALORIES   0 CHOLESTEROL   0 FAT   3 MGS SODIUM

רייז קוגעל

RICE PUDDING

THE JEWISH COOKS FROM EASTERN EUROPE WHO EMIGRATED TO

England in the early part of the twentieth century learned about rice pudding from the locals. True to their culinary roots, the newcomers dubbed it rice kugel. Eating rice kugel was a small step towards fitting in, a constant challenge for these immigrants, whose acceptance in a very old Protestant society depended on shedding their peculiar, un-British ways. The original kind (as even the most inexperienced cook knows) is prepared with whole milk, long-grain white rice, and a carload of sugar. Instead, feast on my dreamy pareve dessert prepared the *Kosher Light* way: using arborio rice, the grain of choice for plump and creamy risotto. Adding low-fat rice milk instead of low-fat cow's milk to the pot completely eliminates cholesterol, cuts down on sodium by more than twenty-five percent, and converts the traditionally milchig dessert to pareve. A light combination (a little goes a long way) of molasses, brown sugar, and a touch of vanilla sweetens this classic dessert. Your taste buds won't know the difference, but your constitution will.

SERVES FOUR

⅜ carton (12 ounces) plain low-fat rice milk (1 ½ cups)

½ cup bottled water

1 teaspoon packed brown sugar

1 ½ teaspoons molasses

¼ teaspoon ground nutmeg

½ teaspoon vanilla extract

4 ounces arborio rice (½ cup)

In a medium, heavy-bottomed pot with a tightly fitting lid, combine the rice milk, bottled water, brown sugar, molasses, nutmeg, and vanilla extract. Stir. Warm the mixture over low heat for 5 minutes, stirring, to dissolve the sugar and molasses, until steam begins to rise.

Add the rice ¼ cup at a time, stirring to combine the rice with the sweetened milk mixture. Raise the heat to medium and bring the mixture to a simmer, stirring occasionally.

Cover the pot and continue to cook at a simmer for 45 minutes, stirring frequently. Don't let the pudding boil. As it cooks, the rice swells to double its original size, absorbing almost all the sweetened milk. The pudding is done when the rice is tender, the texture is thick and creamy, and the color is very soft brown. Yields 2 cups.

Serve mounded in small bowls. Warm or chilled, the rich-tasting rice pudding is yummy.

Rice pudding keeps in the refrigerator for 1 week in an airtight container. If you have any left over, it makes wonderful breakfast fare.

Rice pudding made with rice milk is pareve.

NO GRAIN, NO GAIN: Rice was introduced to the Jews of Babylonia by the conquering Persians twenty-five hundred years ago, and it became ingrained right from the start. Its popularity spread from the Jewish settlements in the Middle East to Sephardic Jewish communities of the Mediterranean where it, too, became a staple. To this day, a Sephardic meal is incomplete without the venerable grain. In fact, the Sephardim can eat rice on Pesach, a food strictly forbidden to the Ashkenazim during the holiday.

ONE SERVING OF RICE PUDDING (ONE-HALF CUP) COOKED KOSHER LIGHT CONTAINS:

 163 CALORIES ♥ 0 CHOLESTEROL 2 GMS FAT 36 MGS SODIUM

HONEY CAKE (LEKACH)

WHILE THE GOLDEN SYRUP OF ROSH HASHANAH IS THE MAIN feature of this *lekach*, it also derives sweetness from freshly squeezed orange juice and raisins rehydrated in a bath of Madeira wine. As you know, coffee is also a common ingredient in honey cake, so use your best bean. Feel free to serve the cake after a festive fleishig meal of chicken or brisket. Patience is the key ingredient in turning out one honey of a *Kosher Light* honey cake. Bake the *lekach* at least one day before you plan to serve it — the morning of the day before is choice — the taste and texture improve tenfold over time. The honey cake miraculously moistens as it sets.

SERVES EIGHT (MAKES ONE LOAF)

2 ounces raisins (¼ cup)	2 ounces egg substitute
¼ cup Madeira wine	1 cup flour
Canola oil spray	1 teaspoon low-sodium baking powder
2 tablespoons pareve unsalted margarine	¼ teaspoon cream of tartar
⅓ cup honey	1 teaspoon ground ginger
1 ½ teaspoons vanilla extract	½ teaspoon ground cinnamon
1 tablespoon freshly squeezed orange juice	¼ teaspoon finely ground coffee

Preheat the oven to 325 degrees.

Quick-spray the bottom and sides of an 8 ½ x 4 ½ x 2 ½-inch loaf pan with canola oil.

Combine the raisins and the wine in a small glass or ceramic bowl. Toss to coat well. Cover and set aside to rehydrate for 1 hour. Give the fruit a second toss after 30 minutes. Transfer the rehydrated fruit into a clean bowl and discard the rehydrating liquid.

Cut the margarine into ½-inch pieces.

Put the margarine, honey, vanilla extract, orange juice, and egg substitute into a food processor or blender. Process to blend.

Sift the flour, baking powder, the cream of tartar, the ginger, the cinnamon, and the coffee together into a medium bowl.

Add the flour mixture to the wet ingredients in the food processor or blender. Process for 2 minutes to blend well. The consistency of the batter is best smooth and creamy. Add the wine-infused raisins to the batter and stir to distribute evenly.

Drop the batter by tablespoonfuls into the loaf pan. Set the loaf pan aside for 2 minutes to let the batter settle before baking.

Place the honey cake into the oven and bake for 30 minutes until it turns a rich golden brown. To test for doneness, insert a toothpick into the center of the cake. If it comes out clean, the *lekach* is ready. Set the cake aside to cool to room temperature.

To remove the honey cake from the loaf pan, run a knife along the sides to loosen it and invert the pan to release the cake. Transfer the *lekach* into an airtight container.

Like a classic fruit cake, the texture of the honey cake improves and its flavor deepens (the cake gains moisture and sweetness), if it's put-up for at least a day before serving. Plan for it — set the *lekach* aside at room temperature for 24 hours.

Use a very sharp knife to slice the cake into 8 pieces, each about 1-inch thick.

Serve the honey cake with tea or coffee following a traditional Rosh Hashanah meal of brisket tzimmes.

The leftover honey cake keeps for up to 2 weeks stored in an airtight container in the refrigerator.

Honey cake is pareve.

ONE SERVING OF HONEY CAKE (ONE SLICE) BAKED KOSHER LIGHT CONTAINS:

 94 CALORIES   0 CHOLESTEROL    2 GMS FAT    11 MGS SODIUM

מצה קוגעל

MATZAH KUGEL

MATZAH PUDDING HAILS FROM THE ANGLO-JEWISH COOKING

tradition. The inspiration was clearly bread pudding, an English favorite born of thriftiness. Motivated by a like sense of economy, you can prepare this recipe during the last few days of Pesach, ensuring that your inevitable matzah surplus is put to good use. The Anglo-Jewish recipe for matzah pudding typically calls for three eggs and a frightening amount of sugar. You can get an equally delicious result by omitting real egg yolks and relying on healthful dried fruits to supplement the scant quarter cup of sugar in my recipe for sweetness.

SERVES EIGHT (MAKES ONE EIGHT-INCH PUDDING)

½ cup Concord grape wine	1 teaspoon ground cinnamon
2 ½ ounces dried figs, chopped (½ cup)	1 teaspoon almond extract
2 ½ ounces golden raisins (½ cup)	1 teaspoon vanilla extract
1 tablespoon pareve unsalted margarine	1 medium Granny Smith apple
4 sodium-free matzahs	1 tablespoon freshly squeezed lemon juice
1 egg white	2 tablespoons slivered almonds
4 ounces egg substitute	1 sheet (18-inch square) parchment paper
¼ cup sugar	½ teaspoon packed brown sugar
	½ teaspoon honey for garnish

Combine the wine, figs, and raisins in a large glass or ceramic bowl. Toss to coat well. Cover and set aside to rehydrate for 1 hour. Give the fruit a second toss after 30 minutes. Transfer the rehydrated fruit into a clean bowl and discard the rehydrating liquid.

In a small skillet, over low heat, melt the margarine. Set aside to cool.

Put the matzahs into a large nonreactive baking pan. Add water to cover, about 5 cups. Set aside to soak for 3 minutes until the matzahs are very soft. Discard the unabsorbed water.

Place half the softened pieces of matzah into a fine-meshed sieve. Press the excess water out of the matzah with the back of a large spoon. Repeat this process for the remaining softened matzah. The drained matzah is the consistency of cooked oatmeal. Yields about 3 cups.

Put the matzah paste into a large bowl. Stir in the melted margarine, egg whites, egg substitute, sugar, cinnamon, almond extract, and vanilla extract. Continue to stir the matzah paste until it thickens to form a stiff batter. Set aside.

Peel and core the apple. Cut it into quarters and coarsely chop. Drizzle the lemon juice over the apple to prevent the flesh from turning brown.

Into the bowl of matzah batter, add the figs, raisins, chopped apple, and almonds. Stir vigorously to distribute the ingredients evenly throughout. Set aside.

Preheat the oven to 325 degrees.

Release the bottom of an 8-inch springform pan from its sides. Trace the bottom onto a sheet of parchment paper and cut out the paper circle. Dampen one side of the circle with a few drops of water. Place it into the bottom of the pan damp-side down. Reassemble the springform pan.

Cut out strips of parchment paper wide enough to cover the sides of the springform pan. Dampen one side of each strip with a few drops of water. Place them, damp-side down, to cover the sides of the pan.

Pour the matzah batter into the springform pan. Gently smooth out the surface of the batter with the back of a teaspoon. Sprinkle the brown sugar over the top of the pudding. Cover the pan with aluminum foil.

Place the matzah pudding into the oven and bake for 50 minutes. Remove the foil and continue to bake for 20 minutes more until the pudding turns a light golden brown. To test for doneness, insert a toothpick into the center of the kugel. If it comes out clean, the matzah pudding is ready. Set it aside to cool to room temperature.

Release the bottom of the springform pan from its sides. Slide the pudding off the pan bottom onto a serving plate. Peel the parchment paper off the sides of the cake.

Garnish the top of the kugel with a drizzle of honey.

Cut the kugel into 8 wedges with a long, very sharp knife. Slip the knife between the bottom of the wedge and the parchment paper and place the individual servings on dessert plates.

Matzah pudding keeps for up to 5 days in an airtight container in the refrigerator.

Matzah kugel is pareve.

MATZAH SCIENCE: On Passover, special round matzah is baked called matzah shmura, meaning "supervised or guarded." Every precaution is taken to prevent the matzah from leavening. The flour is kept bone dry until the water is added to form the dough. The dough is set out for exactly eighteen minutes. (Any longer puts it at risk of fermenting.) The dough is shaped quickly and punched full of tiny holes, a final safeguard against rising. According to Orthodox custom, matzah shmura must be made by a man.

ONE SERVING OF MATZAH KUGEL (ONE SLICE) BAKED KOSHER LIGHT CONTAINS:

 214 CALORIES ♥ 0 CHOLESTEROL 3GMS FAT ▯ 27MGS SODIUM

מאנדל ברויט

MANDELBROIT

MANDELBROIT MEANS ALMOND BREAD, WHICH EXPLAINS WHY
traditional recipes call for one cup of nuts. To cut down on the fat in these twice-baked
cookies, I've really backed off the almonds, but preserved their essence with the extract and
an accent of aromatic spices. The cornmeal keeps you crunching as you munch. The *mandelbroit*
are studded with tiny brandy-flavored currants rather than fleshier raisins. This way, the
fruit doesn't pop out as the cookies bake. This recipe produces super-hard cookies, perfect
for dunking in your favorite teatime beverage (most deliciously coffee).

MAKES EIGHTEEN COOKIES

1 ½ ounces dried currants (¼ cup)   ½ teaspoon vanilla extract

2 tablespoons brandy   1 ½ cups flour

2 ½ tablespoons pareve unsalted margarine   1 teaspoon low-sodium baking powder

½ cup packed brown sugar   ¼ cup cornmeal

2 egg whites   ¼ teaspoon ground cinnamon

½ teaspoon minced lemon zest   ¼ teaspoon ground ginger

1 teaspoon almond extract   1 tablespoon slivered almonds

Combine the currants and the brandy in a small glass or ceramic bowl. Toss to coat well.
Cover and set aside to rehydrate for 1 hour. Give the currants a second toss after 30
minutes. Transfer the rehydrated currants into a clean bowl. Set aside.

Reserve the unabsorbed brandy.

Cut the margarine into ½-inch pieces.

Put the brandy, margarine, brown sugar, egg whites, lemon zest, almond extract, and vanilla extract into a food processor or blender. Process to blend.

Sift the flour, baking powder, cornmeal, cinnamon, and ginger together into a medium bowl.

Add the flour mixture to the wet ingredients in the food processor or blender and process to just combine. The consistency of the batter is best lumpy. Transfer the cookie batter into an airtight container. Cover and set aside to chill in the refrigerator for 2 hours.

Preheat the oven to 375 degrees.

Line a 14 x 16-inch baking sheet with parchment paper.

Remove the dough from the refrigerator and put it on a lightly floured board. Add the currants and the almonds to the dough. Knead the dough to completely incorporate and evenly distribute the currants and the almonds throughout. Shape the dough into a round log, 10 inches long. Tamp down both ends of the log to flatten them. Place the log on the baking sheet.

Bake the *mandelbroit* log in the oven for 35 minutes until it expands slightly, the texture becomes cakelike, and the outside turns toasty brown. Set the log aside for 10 minutes to cool.

Using a very sharp knife, slice the log crosswise into 18 equal-sized cookie rounds a little over ½-inch thick.

Line the baking sheet with a fresh piece of parchment paper. Arrange the *mandelbroit* cookies on the baking sheet spaced ½-inch apart.

Bake in the oven for 15 minutes. Turn the cookies over and continue to bake them for 15 minutes more until they become very hard and turn light golden brown Set the *mandelbroit* aside to cool to room temperature.

Serve this quintessential dunking cookie with fresh-brewed coffee — one might call *mandelbroit* Jewish biscotti, but for their round cookie-like shape.

Mandelbroit keep for weeks in a cookie jar or in an airtight container in the cupboard.

Mandelbroit are pareve.

ONE SERVING OF MANDELBROIT (ONE COOKIE) BAKED KOSHER LIGHT CONTAINS:

 66 CALORIES  0 CHOLESTEROL  2 GMS FAT  6 MGS SODIUM

ACKNOWLEDGMENTS

MY THANKS TO COLLEAGUES, FRIENDS, AND FAMILY WHO HELPED to make *Kosher Light*: at Fly Productions, Esther Mitgang, the brains behind the project, and Maria Mayr, the creator of the book's glorious illustrations; at Penguin Studio, Michael Fragnito, Roni Axelrod, and Sarah Scheffel, for their talent and enthusiasm; my friends Judy Sinclair and Mike Rose, for their invaluable baking advice; Randy Field, for sharing his childhood memories; Shirley Mitgang, for Yiddish, fricassee, and favors; Joan Nathan, for shedding light; at *The Jewish Bulletin of Northern California*, my editors and my outspoken readership; and my parents, Ezekiel and Ophira Bahar, my mother-in-law, Mary Vaccaro, my siblings, Iris, Ron, and Laurie, and my brother-in-law, Andrew Gabor.

My special acknowledgment to the authors of: *The Jewish Holiday Kitchen* by Joan Nathan, *In Search of Plenty* by Oded Schwartz, *The New Complete International Jewish Cookbook* by Evelyn Rose, and *The Book of Jewish Food* by Claudia Rosen, for the useful information I discovered in their books.